INSTRUCTOR'S MANUAL FOR

THE SOCIAL WORK INTERVIEW

A Guide for Human Service Professionals

Alfred Kadushin
Goldie Kadushin

Fourth Edition

Columbia University Press   New York

Columbia University Press
Publishers Since 1893
New York   Chichester, West Sussex
Copyright © 1997 Columbia University Press
All rights reserved

Library of Congress Cataloging-in-Publication Data
Kadushin, Alfred.
    Instructor's manual for the social work interview
Alfred Kadushin, Goldie Kadushin. — 4th ed.
        p.   cm.
    Includes bibliographical references and index.
    ISBN 0-231-10847-8 (pbk.)
    1. Interviewing. 2. Social service. I. Kadushin, Goldie.
II. Title.

♾   CIP

Casebound editions of Columbia University Press books are printed
on permanent and durable acid-free paper.

Printed in the United States of America

c 10 9 8 7 6 5 4 3 2 1

Contents

On Teaching and Learning

We hope that instructors representing a number of different but related disciplines—social workers, counselors, psychologists, teachers, and others—have used and will use this book. Each group has had somewhat different educational objectives in using the text. Each instructor may have used the text differently, emphasizing different learning outcomes. Consequently, it did not seem desirable to organize an instructor's manual in terms of educational objectives for each unit. You the instructor will know best how you will want to use the text material.

It seemed more useful to organize an instructor's handbook in terms of suggested structured learning experiences, class exercises, that you can use to help students learn more effectively. The handbook also offers suggestions for semester assignments and examinations for evaluating students' performance. Thus we have designed the instructor's manual as a compendium of suggested structured learning experiences, teaching aids and assignments, and examination questions. We trust that you will modify and adapt this material to suit your needs and class situation.

Instructors generally have a preferred emphasis in their approach to teaching. Some are cognitively oriented, emphasizing the teaching of concepts, principles, theory, and related knowledge. Others are oriented to skills and performance, emphasizing changing behavior through practice. Others are affectively oriented, attempting to develop change in attitudes and feelings. Perhaps most instructors are eclectic, emphasizing the approach most congruent and appropriate to the content they are teaching. However, it is generally thought the best way to instruct professionals is in the context of analyzing professional problems similar to those in which students will ultimately have to use their knowledge.

Every instructor knows, or soon learns, that structured experiences, teaching aids, assignments, and exams offer limited learning in and of themselves. What they primarily provide are the stimuli for learning, but instructors need to direct and use such stimuli to facilitate and make learning conscious and explicit. Structured experiences, exercises, and exams provide an opportunity for learning. The instructor has to help the student take optimum advantage of the opportunity presented by these resources.

The general principles and procedures identified as facilitating effective teaching-learning are, of course, applicable to the teaching of interviewing:

1. Teachers have to have an expert knowledge and understanding of the subject matter and be motivated to share this knowledge. However egalitarian their conduct of the class, the responsibility for subject-matter expertise suggests an inherent inequality. Students can legitimately expect that teachers will know more about interviewing than they do and that they can look to their teachers for answers or for guidance in finding answers.

Someone once said that the difference between the scholar and the teacher is that the scholar knows the subject matter but is not particularly interested in communicating this knowledge. The teacher, on the other hand, not only knows the subject matter but is much interested in communicating it to others.

2. Teachers have to prepare for each class meeting. This means that teachers have to know what they hope to teach in each session, know how they hope to teach it, and how this relates to preceding and subsequent class meetings. Knowing the subject-matter content is not enough. Teachers have to systematically organize the content for meaningful presentation.

If we view the total course as a play with a beginning, middle, and end, each class meeting is a different act in the play. And, as in a play, each act contributes in a logical sequential progression to achieving the overall objective of the play. This requires careful preparation for each class meeting.

3. Because no two class groups are alike, teachers have to be flexible and adaptable. What was a howling success and clearly effective with one group may prove only marginally useful with another class. Teachers

have to be willing to solicit student feedback and make changes in response to such feedback.

Instructors have to be situationally responsive. Monitoring feedback from the class and being sensitive to the changing atmosphere of the class enables instructors to exploit the teaching-learning potential of whatever happens in class.

Teachers can only teach. They cannot ensure learning. Only the student can learn. All learning is ultimately self-education. But a thorough knowledge of the subject matter; careful organization of the course content; responsible preparation for each class meeting; an attitudinal and behavioral approach to students that communicates respect, acceptance, and stimulation of their involvement; reasonable adherence to validated principles of teaching—all add up to facilitation of learning. If only the learner can learn and the teacher can only teach, the teacher can maximize the facilitation of learning. Teaching, then, is the art of helping others to learn.

4. Students learn best when they are actively involved in the learning experience. The teacher has to maximize such involvement. At the very least this requires that the teacher accept attitudinally the desirability of student participation and involvement. The teacher has to be able, willing, and ready to share authority, decisional prerogatives, and class time with the student.

5. Students learn best if they can devote as much of their emotional energies as possible to learning. Emotional energy devoted to defending themselves from attack, loss of self-esteem, and derogation is energy robbed from learning. Thus a teacher who generates a class atmosphere of psychological safety, who can be counted on to be sensitive to a student's need for support, provides a context that facilitates learning.

There is, if not a contradiction, at least a dilemma here. Learning is not likely to take place unless students are willing to expose, explore, and identify their difficulties, inadequacies, and failures in interviewing. Learning involves risk and the willingness to accept risk. The interviewing class is not a safe place. But such risks are more likely to be incurred and accepted if students have a feeling that their teachers will compassionately accept and support students when, and if, they display their ignorance. Any feeling they will be ridiculed, derogated, or punished is apt to seriously inhibit learning.

One difficulty derives from the antithetical demands on the instructor to be both teacher and evaluator of student performance. The instructor not only has to be compassionate, accepting, and understanding but must at the same time make demands and critically evaluate student performance. The teacher must communicate clear expectations that students will consistently and conscientiously work in learning the subject matter. Failure to achieve the learning and changes required for passing the course calls for a failing grade—if we are to be fair to the other students who have mastered course content and ultimately to the client who has the right to be competently interviewed. Adherence to standards requires that we certify students not because we have no evidence of incompetence but because we have evidence of interviewing competence.

6. A student learns best if the teacher takes into consideration the student's uniqueness as a learner.

Stated differently, this is a call to individualize the learner, to start where the learner is. This is difficult in classroom teaching. The unit of attention is the class group rather than the individual student. An approach that is best for student A is less desirable for student B. There is no way, in teaching a group, to select an approach to teaching that best meets the individual learning preferences of each student.

However, teachers can be aware that the class is composed of people who have different patterns of learning, who respond with feelings to the way the teacher organizes the class and teaches the content. Some students feel comfortable with highly structured and clearly organized learning contexts, and others chafe under the control this implies, preferring a more open, free-flowing, unstructured learning context.

Some cannot engage in experiential learning situations until they have some prior didactic review of what it is they are supposed to be doing. And some cannot learn the didactic material until they have had the opportunity for an experiential encounter. Some students are compliant, drinking in the material, capturing it uncritically in their notebooks. Some are anxious, dependent, primarily concerned with course requirements and grades, and learn only what they think will be on the exam. Some are attention seekers, using the classroom situation as a stage to obtain periodic reinforcement from others about their likability. Some students are contentiously independent, critically chewing over the material in their minds, accepting it only when they can integrate it with what they already know. Different people, different kinds of learners. Teachers aware of the heterogeneity of the group have to monitor class feedback to see whether they are meeting the learning needs of at least a majority of the class. In addition to this, teachers may want to consider what opportunities may exist for individualizing the teaching-learning situation. A course in interviewing may offer more such opportunities than a large lecture course in geology, for instance.

At the very least, the teacher can seek to learn the names of students in the group. This individualizes students when the teacher calls on them. So does referring to the student by name in using the student's contribution to the discussion: "As Bill said a little while ago . . ."

7. Students learn best if content is meaningfully presented.

Teaching that is planned in terms of continuity (reiteration of important content—deepening learning), sequence (successively building toward greater complexity—broadening learning), and integration (relating different content to each other) is teaching presented in a more meaningful context.

Content is meaningfully presented if it fits into some general theoretical framework. The teacher has to have some cognitive map of the whole interviewing process—some model, some design—that helps to organize the content.

Content is meaningfully presented if it is selective. Not everything is of equal importance, and some content deserves more time and more emphasis than others.

Imaginative repetition makes learning more meaningful. If we select a number of different experiences that teach the same idea in different ways, that idea is easier to grasp and accept. Through comparison and contrast, illustrations of similarities and differences, the same content is more meaningfully presented.

Learning is more meaningful if it can be made conscious and explicit. We are not always aware of what of it is that we have learned. To the extent that we can consciously articulate and label what we have learned, the learning is apt to be more meaningful and transferable. This calls attention to the need for periodic recapitulation and summarizing of content.

8. Students learn best when learning is followed by positive satisfaction. Positive feedback, praise, is psychic satisfaction that teachers can liberally dispense in response to improvements in performance. Indiscriminate praise is, of course, counterproductive. Offer praise only when the student's work warrants it.

Teachers have some responsibility for organizing the learning situation in a way that increases the probability of success in learning. Success in learning is perhaps the most significant positive satisfaction that a student can experience. We ensure the probability of successful learning by organizing the presentation so that the student moves from familiar content to the unfamiliar new content. We ensure the probability of successful learning if we offer the content to be learned in digestible dosages. We ensure the probability of successful learning if we move in logical progression from the simple to the complex. We ensure probability of success if we make learning demands that are within the student's capacity at any given time.

We can reduce the potency of the dissatisfaction that comes from failure by preparing for failure. We share with students that much of this is difficult and that they might fail on their first attempts.

9. Students learn best if they are highly motivated to learn.

The teacher's responsibility then is to nurture and enhance the motivation students bring to the course. Where students' motivation is limited, the teacher's responsibility is to stimulate and develop their motivation. Thus students who register for the course because they need two or three extra credits, or because the course is given at a convenient time, may need motivation to learn interviewing. Students who already regard themselves as experienced hot-shot interviewers with little that they need to learn are, once again, not motivated to invest time or effort in the course. Even if satisfied with students' interviewing skills, the teacher may have to stimulate their motivation by confronting students with the gap between what they are doing and what more needs to be done, with some shortcomings in their performance.

We can increase motivation by explaining to students the relevance of the content to be taught. This is comparatively easy in a course in interviewing. The utility and significance of most of the content is self-evident. It is useful for aspiring social workers, journalists, psychologists, lawyers, and doctors.

But the value of all the content is not so self-evident. We can increase motivation if we explain the usefulness and meaningfulness of the content.

Students may not, for instance, be motivated to learn about the process of interpersonal communication. Explaining how learning the key concepts of interpersonal communication will enable them to increase their interviewing skills increases students' motivation to learn these concepts. We increase motivation to learn content for which students have low learning motivation by tying this content to areas of high motivation.

In Apologia

As we reviewed the material in the introduction in revising the manual for the fourth edition, we became uneasy that the statement of principles of teaching-learning might appear presumptuous. After all, people who are teaching now know a lot about teaching and how to go about it. You don't need somebody to tell you. But, then, as we reread it a fourth or fifth time, we thought that although it might tell you what you already know, the explicitness with which it presents teaching principles might be helpful and serve as a reminder of things we need to remember. So we left it in.

Resources for Instruction

Audiovisual Aids

The third edition of the handbook had a twenty-eight–page listing of audiovisual aid resources for instruction. The listing included audiotapes, movies, videotapes, and such that demonstrated some aspect of interviewing developed for human services personnel.

In the eight years that have elapsed since the last edition this—and many other items in the previous listing—regretfully became archaic or unavailable.

Rather than update the relevant audiovisual resources available, we have decided to include a listing of directories that catalogue such resources. Each directory includes a short summary of each item, source, availability, format, length, cost, and the like. These indexes are updated frequently to ensure currency:

1. Teri Kessler Schell, ed. *The Video Source Book*, 17th ed., 2 vols. New York: Gale Research, 1996 (3,296 pp.).
2. *Education Film and Video Locator of the Consortium of College and University Media Centers*,, 4th ed., 2 vols. New York: R. R. Bowker, 1991–1992 (3,361 pp.).
3. C. Edward Wall, ed. *Media Review Digest*, vol. 25. Ann Arbor, Mich.: Pierian Press, 1995 (1,048 pp.).
4. Charles M. Murtaugh, ed. *1987 Directory of Medical Audio/Visual Programs for the Health Sciences and Related Fields*. Hawthorne, N.J.: Med/Av Publishing, 1987.

Structured Experiences: Classroom Exercises

In using structured learning experiences—movies, tapes, role-playing, class experiences—some considerations need to be explicit.

Teaching interviewing skills follows the logical progression of (1) presenting the skill to be learned—didactically or through modeling, or both; (2) giving the student the opportunity to practice the skill by using it in a natural or simulated situation; (3) providing feedback that rewards what the student did correctly and effectively and identifies what the student needs to change; (4) practicing and using the skill once again, this time with an effort to make the changes recommended; (5) evaluating and giving feedback about this second attempt.

Learning from structured experiences in the class group is maximized if instructor and students follow a cycle:

1. Students participate in the experience.
2. Students share their experiences and discuss them in the group.
3. As a consequence of the discussion, students identify some ideas, generalizations, principles, and guidelines around some aspect of interviewing.
4. Students attempt to apply what they have learned to another structured experience, and the cycle begins again.

Technically, what is involved is a process of inductive learning—from the experience to the generalization.

Students need to process the group feedback if they are to explicitly identify what they are learning. Searching for recurrent themes in the statements of the group, listing recurrent adjectives or recurrent problems on the board, the instructor then attempts to link the experience of group members to some theory or generalization. This links the experience of this group to experiences of others outside the group. It tests the validity of what this group of students has found. It helps answer this question: "What have I learned that has validity?"

In stimulating students to share their experience the instructor asks such questions as

What did you observe?
How did you feel?
How did you react behaviorally?
What did you think of doing differently?
What would you have preferred?
Could you be more specific?
How could you have said that differently?

In helping the group process the experience the instructor asks questions such as

Who had the same experience?
How was it different for you?
How many felt the same way about that?
What surprised you in the exercise?
How would you explain that?

In generalizing from the experience the instructor asks such questions as

What was significant about this?
What meaning does it have for you?
How do you fit it together?
What seems to be operating here?
What theoretical idea does this seem to illustrate?
What do you know of research relating to this?
How does this relate to other things you know about interviewing?

In selecting an exercise you should be mindful of certain considerations in addition to learning objectives. One is the level of readiness and sophistication of the group. Some groups may find some exercises strange, artificial, and an imposition on their privacy. Some exercises may be acceptable once members of the group have become familiar with each other but may be unacceptable early in the process of group formation. Some individual group members may be reluctant to participate and should not be coerced. Participation should be, to the greatest extent possible, voluntary.

One danger is that the exercise itself may become the focus of attention and concern. This would be counterproductive. The purpose and focus of the exercise is to stimulate learning. The exercise is a vehicle for learning rather than an end in itself.

Learning exercises, as compared with listening to lectures, increase the risk of failure and self-disclosure and require greater interpersonal interaction with others. As a consequence, students are apt to have greater anxiety with such learning formats and pose greater resistance to participating.

All class exercises and group discussion involve elements of threat, competition, demand, expectation, and sometimes mild embarrassment. This may be particularly true for those students who have never before participated in role-playing or videotaping. Consequently, although an accepting, respectful, and supportive atmosphere is always a desirable approach to teaching-learning, it is particularly important in conducting the exercises.

Students will find that the exercises, role-playing, and videotaping are interesting, stimulate a high level of participation, and are the nearest thing to the real thing that we can make available in class. Exercises provide students with an experience that illustrates, exemplifies, or simulates the interaction of a real-life situation. These rewards serve to balance the threat and embarrassment that students may fear.

Structured experiences mobilize energies and focus them on the learning tasks. After participating in such exercises, discussing them critically, and identifying some ideas they derived from the exercise, students are apt to feel a greater sense of "ownership" in their learning. Involvement and participation give their learning a greater sense of immediacy than being at the receiving end of a didactic lecture.

Research indicates that using structured learning experiences also has the advantage of developing greater group cohesiveness and a more positive perception of the instructor by the group.

In providing instructional experiences the instructor increases the possibilities for self-learning and distributes greater responsibility for learning to the student. The structured experience rather than the instructor becomes the source and medium of learning. The structured experience requires that students behave in some defined way—observing, talking, or acting.

As the instructor you still have considerable responsibility in selecting the experience in which the student will become involved. This selection requires that you know clearly what the teaching objectives are and how the experience selected will help achieve the explicit teaching objective. You are responsible for clearly interpreting what students are being asked to do and for organizing the exercise.

But even more significant is that the instructor is responsible for helping make the exercise educationally productive. Doing the exercise is only the beginning. You have to help students share their response to the experience, integrating this with their previous learning, generalizing from the experience, and linking the experience to theory so that students formulate broader principles for action and apply what they learned to effective interviewing.

You may find it profitable to precede the exercise with a small lecture that reveals your reasons for choosing the exercise and how it fits into the total course. Instructors can follow up with another short lecture in which they make explicit what the group might have learned from the experience. Much is being asked of students as well as the instructor, both before and after the exercise.

Early in the course, before students get to know each other and the instructor, it is easier for class members to analyze and critique interviews in which they have not been personally involved. Later in the course, after group members are more comfortable with each other and with the instructor, it is more psychologically appropriate to ask students themselves to engage in exercises for group analysis and critique.

Thus the instructor starts by using typescripts, movies, audio and videotapes of interviewing by strangers—nonclass members. Students find these experiences less threatening to view objectively and to critique vigorously. Only after such introductory experiences, and after the class has developed as a group, can the instructor ask that students play a role in a mock interview for class observation and analysis.

This sequence of experiences has relevance to a second progression regarding the introduction of interviewing cues for analysis. Moving from the simple to the more complex, you should limit class analysis of first interviews to content cues. A typescript of an interview presents the content of the interview without the audio or visual cues. Moving from typescripts to audiotapes increases the cues by adding aural-vocal cues to content cues—voice, inflection, intonation, pauses, silences, and the like. Moving from audiotapes to videotapes adds visual nonverbal behavioral cues to the aural cues that were added to the content cues. Moving from videotape to role-playing adds immediate contextual cues to the visual, aural, and content cues.

The amount of detail available for analysis in the live interview is overwhelming. Instructors must introduce such detail gradually and sequentially in a controlled manner.

Structured Experiences

Role Playing

Because interviewing courses frequently use role-playing, it requires some extended comment.

Mock interviews are flexible.[*] Instructors can vary the content to emphasize different problems, focus on specific skills, and point up different learnings. It all depends on the imagination you as the instructor bring to incorporating the selected elements in the role descriptions and staging.

Mock interviews can run for any length of time—five minutes if limited time is available or for twenty minutes.

Role-playing is immediate and real, as contrasted with watching movies or videotapes, which are in the past and another location. Role-playing means direct participation in the event, whereas movies or videotapes involve vicarious participation. Because of its immediacy role-playing has a credibility that few other exercises achieve. As a matter of fact, one problematic aspect of role-playing is that it may become too real for some participants. They lose the sense of difference between role-playing and a real-life encounter and may inadvertently disclose too much about their personal problems. As the instructor you are responsible for protecting such students from too much self-exposure to the group, an exposure they are subsequently likely to regret. If you sense this is happening, you might intervene in the role-playing and redirect it by a question or comment.

Role-playing provides the opportunity to practice and integrate new skills in a protected context. There is no threat of harm to a client because of mistakes that result from inexperience. The immediate feedback from knowledgeable observers provides reinforcement of things well done, explicit identification of errors, and directions in correcting errors. In playing clients' roles students develop a greater empathy with clients' situations.

Role-playing requires the student's participation and involvement. It demands considerable personal exposure. Consequently, you need to ensure that mock interviews are conducted with some care and sensitivity to the possibility of ego bruising. Students are only thinly protected by the agreed-upon fiction that they are merely acting someone else's behavior.

Because role-playing risks self-exposure, it is easier to introduce this

---

[*]We should note that the term for the experience, *role-playing*, does some disservice to its seriousness. Although it is "play," these interactions generate real emotions, and participants manifest real attitudes. If reasonably well structured, role-playing becomes a real experience, far from trivial.

learning experience in a privately performed dyadic context. The group breaks into pairs, a member of the dyad takes an assigned role, and the two enact the roles privately in interaction with each other. The instructor gives the same role-playing assignment to each dyad. Afterward students reconvene as a group and share, compare, and contrast their experiences in enacting the same role situation.

After a number of such experiences (which may involve groups of three or four students, depending on the script) the instructor should solicit volunteers to role-play an interview before the entire class. The role-playing then becomes a basis for group discussion. The most productive procedure involves videotaping the role-playing for immediate stop-start playback for critique and discussion.

Throughout, the teacher needs to take the initiative in introducing role-playing, even before asking the class to actually participate. A student might ask, "Well, how do you get the interview properly started?" You might respond by saying, "Well, let's suppose someone—anyone—in the class has just come into my office for a scheduled interview. The telephone intake note tells me that this is an interviewee who is requesting help regarding day care for children. I will be the interviewer, and let's role-play the first minute or so of the interview."

The teacher may be the first to volunteer to role-play an interview in front of the group and videotape it for feedback from the group.

This suggests that here, as elsewhere, the instructor has to have some clear idea of the learning objectives or objectives of the role-playing. What does the instructor hope students will learn from the experience?

In line with this the instructor may write the script. We list here a number of brief descriptions of situations relevant to social work that have been used in classes in social work interviewing. Alternatively, and particularly in the dyadic role-playing situations, the instructor might ask each pair to select a situation that reflects a problem that they have encountered.

If students are to select the problem to be role-played, it might be well to instruct them that the problem should be one that (1) they have experienced personally or vicariously; (2) is a matter of some concern to them; (3) they have unsuccessfully attempted to solve on their own; (4) and that they feel a strong desire to resolve.

Students often find it helpful for the instructor to offer some topics for the first mock interviews—work experience, reasons for taking the course, hobbies, educational experience, travel experience, the ideal vacation, ideas about the ideal family, and so on.

Sometimes instructors break the class into groups of three with different assignments to each of the three participants—one as interviewee, one as interviewer, the third as objective observer of the role-playing.

Whether in groups of two or three, students can rotate their assignments. Interviewee becomes interviewer, interviewer becomes interviewee, or either one of them takes the role of observer, who then takes the role of an active interview participant.

The script, the problem situation, may remain constant, but the players may be assigned different interviewing approaches to play out their helping role. One interviewer may be assigned an approach that centers on actively offering advice. Another may be assigned to role-play an interviewer whose approach focuses on clarifying alternatives. Or the student interviewer might be assigned to display different attitudes and to focus on eliciting interviewees' reactions—the same situation is enacted with an accepting interested interviewer and alternatively by a bored indifferent hostile interviewer.

The same scripts may focus on problems relating to different kinds of interviewees—the garrulous interviewee; the reticent, resistive, monosyllabic interviewee; the hostile aggressive interviewee.

Scripts formulated by the instructor should provide just enough detail to be useful. Too much detail can restrict spontaneity of responses; too little detail leaves participants to puzzle out many important elements.

Players should be free to improvise, adding data consistent with the general outlines of the role they are playing, but they should be told not to alter the general spirit and direction of the role-playing. The statement should include a role profile for each participant.

After receiving the role, players should have an opportunity to become familiar with the role, to "think" themselves into the role. They also should have an opportunity to ask the instructor any questions they might have about the role-playing and to clarify any ambiguities.

A danger of role-playing is that if it is too broadly enacted—if the role becomes a caricature—the players may reinforce stereotypes. Consequently, the teacher might instruct them to avoid this kind of acting and to play it naturally.

Because any human interaction sustained even for a limited period is highly complex, the instructor may need to simplify the structure of observation. When a group observes role-playing, some members may be designated to identify with and concentrate on the interviewer, the others to identify with and observe the interviewee. On other occasions the instructor may tell the class to concentrate on some specific aspect of the interview—nonverbal behavior, or the nature of transitions, or question formulation.

Observers might use the guide to interview observations listed on page 000 of this manual to focus on significant aspects of the mock interview.

Both because of limited class time and considerations relating to the process of role-playing, it is desirable to restrict the enactments to fifteen to twenty minutes.

Although fifteen to twenty minutes is the outside length, you should terminate an interview sooner if it is becoming boring, losing the attention and involvement of the group, or clearly is diverging from the intended learning objectives. During role-playing you should be available only as a resource person.

Less than fifteen minutes does not permit any feeling of involvement to develop and may not provide enough content for discussion. More than twenty to twenty-five minutes may not permit adequate time for discussion. Role-playing that is not followed by discussion and feedback—either by members of the dyad to each other or by the group to the role-players—robs the experience of a good deal of its potential for learning. So the instructor must guard time carefully and allocate it so that it maximizes learning.

You should inform the group in advance of the time allotted for role-playing and might sound a preliminary warning two or three minutes before the end: "It would help if you could come to a closure in a couple of minutes"; "Would you please try to wrap this up shortly?"

The teacher has the responsibility for structuring the discussion of the role-playing. Consequently, you need to give some thought in advance to the kinds of questions that would direct the group's attention and focus on the content you are hoping students will learn at this point in the course.

Any discussion of a mock interview may need to start with an unstructured debriefing. This involves asking the role-playing participants for any general reactions to the procedure, anything they like to say or ask about their experience. You can offer the players some protection in the discussion, telling them, for example, to maintain their role-playing identities. Thus everyone refers to Sue, the student who played the role of Mrs. Wall, as "Mrs. Wall" during the discussion, not "Sue."

The discussion should have two different but related focuses, one centering on what was said and done and how it was said and done—the overt interview—and the second centering on the introspective emotional responses of the participants to what was said and done—the covert interview. In actual interviews we can only guess at and make inferences about what the interviewee is thinking and feeling in response to what the interviewer did. The discussion of role-playing may provide an unequaled opportunity to see ourselves as others see us—if the participants can be frank and open with each other during the post-role-playing discussion.

In offering feedback the emphasis is on being descriptive and specific rather than evaluative. Class members should give feedback in the form of a question to the role-player rather than as a declarative statement. "At one point in the interview you said [*specifically describing what was said*]. What led you to say that at that point?"

The advantage of retrospective analysis of role-playing is that the participants can share how they felt in response to what their interview partner said or did. They can articulate the aspects of the interview that are hidden. The instructor might ask such questions as, "How did you feel when he said that?"; "What did you hope he would say or do in response to what you said?"; "What went on inside yourself that led you to make that statement?"

At the same time you can point out clearly the things that the participants truly did well, encouraging positive feedback from the class as well. Initiating role-playing by an example of rigorous and balanced criticism sets the stage for and sanctions the pattern of such an approach to all performances.

The most difficult aspect of role-playing for the instructor is to stimulate frank assessment of the interview by the single observer or the class. Students are reluctant to criticize each other, particularly if they sense that in doing so they will be setting a pattern that may make them vulnerable when their role-playing is observed. At the same time they want frank criticism to help them to improve and are impatient with pablum in uncritical discussions. Wanting and fearing critical feedback, they need the help and support of the instructor.

One approach that might be helpful involves risks for the instructor. You take the role of interviewer in the first mock interview. You then provides a self-critique, discussing the role-playing openly and frankly, pointing out the mistakes made (there always are some, if not many), and encouraging students (who will be timid about doing this) to identify and share examples of your poor performance as interviewer.

Role-playing is, of course, not the real thing, and the instructor needs to be explicit about the differences. The transition from mock interviewing to doing an interview with an actual client is not all that automatic.

Instructors can provides scripts for mock interviews in a variety of different ways to demonstrate the varieties of formats. However the script is prepared, it should contain, at minimum, some specific information regarding the interviewer and interviewee. Role-players need to know what kind of agency they represent and whether they have had previous contact with the interviewee. The role-player also needs to know the purpose of this interview.

The script should also contain some specific identifying information regarding the interviewee—child or adult; married or unmarried; if married, any children, their ages, and current living situation; as well as some information about housing and employment. The script should clearly identify the nature of the problem that brings the client to the agency and provide some information about antecedents of the problem and expectations of help from the agency.

The information that sets the stage for a role-playing may be typed on 3 × 5 cards and distributed to the participants. If the group watches the interview, the entire group is informed of the details.

1. Friendship Club

SETTING: A friendship club for the elderly during a weekly lunch program.

INTERVIEWEE: An 80-year-old woman. She is touched daily by the hospitalization of increasing numbers of her friends. She has a hip ailment and has great difficulty with transportation, having to rely on public door-to-door services. She has a married daughter in town on whom she does not like to be too dependent. She enjoys her daughter and grandchildren, but she needs to be with peers who share similar problems. She is willing to talk about her life and situation with anyone who will listen. She often approaches the volunteers at the lunch program because they don't talk about their troubles in return; they listen to her.

INTERVIEW: This is an informal interview in the sense that it is not pre-planned. The interviewer is a volunteer at the lunch program, and the interviewee approaches the volunteer during lunch, feeling the need to talk because she has not been able to get out in a week.

2. Foster Parent Applicants

SETTING: The county department of public welfare, which has responsibility for recruiting and assessing foster family homes for children.

INTERVIEWEE: A 56-year-old woman, Margo Smith, who has applied to become a foster parent. She is married, and her husband John Smith is 58 and works as a butcher for a food manufacturer. The couple has a son and daughter, 28 and 26, both of whom are married and live elsewhere. The couple lives in an old frame house on the east side of town near the food plant.

INTERVIEW: The purpose of the interview is twofold: to obtain information about the family relevant to the foster care application so that the agency can make a reasoned decision, and to provide information about the program that would help the family decide whether to push its application for a foster child.

3. Separation or Divorce

INTERVIEWER INFORMATION: You are a social worker at a county mental health clinic. Your client is Janetta Towne, 45. She has come to your agency because she wants to clarify her decision about seeking a separation or divorce.

CLIENT INFORMATION: You are Janetta Towne, 45, and you have come to see a social worker in a county mental health clinic to discuss the possibility of separating from or divorcing your husband.

You and your husband, an insurance salesman, have been married for twenty-five years. You have two children: your son, 22, is self-supporting, married, and living outside the home; your daughter is a senior in high school. Your husband had a heart attack six months ago and is slowly recovering. He has recently returned to work on a part-time basis. However, he has been irritable since his heart attack and consequently difficult to live with. He complains constantly about everything and is always criticizing you. You have decided you can't take it anymore and would rather separate from or divorce him.

You have a part-time job as a computer programmer that you really enjoy. In fact, your boss has indicated that he would like to have you work full time and take on additional responsibilities, with a raise in salary. This is appealing to you.

You came to this agency once before, eight years ago, for marriage counseling. However, your husband would come to only one session because he refused to see that anything was wrong with the marriage. Your marriage has grown worse since then and now you feel it is beyond saving.

4. Plans for Baby

CAST: Social worker with county department of social services. Susan, 16-year-old mother of 5-month-old son Peter.

BACKGROUND INFORMATION: Susan has been involved with a county social worker since age 11. She is a neglected child herself. Her mother, Selena Sands, left Susan alone for long stretches of time, neglected her physical care, and other primary parenting functions. Susan learned at a young age to call the shots in her life. She was placed in foster care at age 11, remained in care to age 13, then returned home at her own request, and soon became unmanageable. She was truant (missing two to three days a week), unkempt, and began running away. She again was placed in a foster home, but Susan remained truant and continued to run. She then was placed in a group home from which she ran many times. At age 15 Susan became pregnant and was ordered to a residential treatment center that specializes in pregnant teens. In the first two months of placement Susan was present for eight days and on the run the remainder of the time. During her final run she found a woman who wanted to be her foster mother. The woman was duly licensed, and Susan remained with her one and one-half months. She returned to her mother's and at her mother's insistence had the baby and kept the child. She remained at her mother's for six months. In the past eight weeks Susan has moved with the baby to six different locations. Most recently, she left baby with her mother and took off alone. The grandmother, Selena Sands, requested foster placement of the baby.

CURRENT SITUATION: Baby is in foster home on emergency court order. A petition alleging neglect of baby is on file with the court.

PURPOSE OF INTERVIEW: To discuss with Susan the impending court hearing and its implications. To discuss Susan's plans for baby and the court's alternatives.

SETTING: Social worker's office—small with desk and two chairs. Not grossly austere but certainly not inviting.

RELATIONSHIPS: This worker has been involved with Susan for one year, beginning with the court-ordered residential treatment center. Worker and Susan get along reasonably well.

5. Who Is Joan?

I am a worker in an adoption agency. The interviewee is a 28-year-old woman named Joan Block who is requesting information regarding her biological parents. Since her adoptive mother passed away last year, she has felt a need to know more about her roots. She is expecting her second child this summer and would like to be able to give her children more information regarding their heritage. Joan has never been close to her adoptive father because he was almost 40 at the time of the adoption and never took much interest in her care.

Joan lives with her husband and 4-year-old son in a middle-class subur-ban home in Glendale. She is unemployed but has a teaching degree. Her husband is an accountant in a Milwaukee firm.

The policy at our agency is to give the client as much nonidentifying information as we can. State law requires that the individual go through the courts to get any identifying information regarding the biological parents.

6. Child Neglect

Marion Jones, 24, is the mother of three: Matt, 4 years, 8 months; Mindy, 2 years, 3 months; and Mike Jr., 17 months. The children are in her custody, although she has been reported to Children's Protective Services because of severe neglect.

On August 2, 1996, police were called to the Jones home by neighbors who reported that the children had been left alone in the home for two or three "days and nights." When police entered the home, all three children were watching TV. They were dirty and had strong odors, particularly the youngest. Piles of soiled diapers and spoiling food added to the foul smell of the home. Police found Marion Jones unconscious in an upstairs bedroom, the room littered with liquor bottles. Then her sister arrived and took charge. Police took no action other than immediately notifying our agency.

By neighbor's report, Marion Jones is a good housekeeper and mother when she is sober. Neighbors also report that her heavy drinking began about six months after her husband ran off. Before the August 2 incident reported by police officials, our agency had no contact with this family.

Marion Jones states that since her divorce two years ago, she has had little time for herself, that she wants "more space" so that she can start rebuilding her life. She wants to upgrade her employment skills because she believes her chances of remarrying are slim with three kids, and she is "sick of welfare." She thinks she still loves her three children but sometimes finds herself angry and yelling and hitting them. She frequently feels that they are "in the way."

Marion Jones wants to cure her drinking problem. She wants to work on her emotions so she "won't feel rotten all the time." She also wants to work a job and a half so that she can get her bills caught up and "have some extra money to spend on the children."

She is requesting foster home placement for her three children.

INTERVIEWER: Although you believe that foster care might be the best arrangement for the Jones family, your agency has a policy of keeping families intact and considers foster care a last resort.

Your task as worker is to help Marion Jones choose what's best for her among available options, so that she can begin the rehabilitation and recovery process.

7. Confrontation

AGENCY: Program for Assertive Community Treatment (PACT), a mental health agency that treats chronically mentally ill people in the community. A major focus is on functional living skills such as employment.

CLIENT: Jim, 24, has been in PACT for 2.5 years, diagnosed as schizophrenic. Psychiatric difficulties began four years ago, when he was a university student and into drugs. I have been meeting with Jim since early November once a week at his apartment. Our contacts have been for the purpose of emotional support and for problem solving involving issues that have come up—paying bills, being able to set limits with his friends when they try to take advantage of him, and so forth. Jim has a great deal of trouble being straightforward with people. He is not able to express how he is feeling and often gives the impression that things are fine when they are not. He will agree with anything you say and lies quite frequently, usually to cover up a failure on his part.

FOCUS OF INTERVIEW: Jim had been working until Christmas at a local cheese-processing plant and at another similar job before that. He has been out of work since Christmas and has expressed interest in getting some job training in the janitorial department at Goodwill Industries. Jim was accepted into the program but only showed up twice the first week and once the second. When his attendance did not improve the third week, Jim was dropped from the program. I asked Jim to call Goodwill to determine his status, and he told me that he would be given a chance again the next week. He had also told his parents that things were going well at work. He had lied several times during the past three weeks to staff members about having been to work on days that he wasn't at work.

PURPOSE OF INTERVIEW: To confront Jim with my knowledge that he's been lying; to explore the reasons for and dynamics of the situation in which he lies; to identify the reasons for not showing up at Goodwill; to offer support.

8. Client in Trouble

Instruct a student to play the role of a young client who has been referred to a social worker by the court. The client has been reported for shoplifting. The client is ambiguous about the referral and resists the social worker's effort to discuss the incident.

Have other students in the class briefly interview the client in turn, illustrating their approaches to induce the client to talk.

Play the interviews out in front of the entire group. Lead a discussion of which approach seems most effective and of the similarities and differences in approaches used.

The role-playing client shares her reactions to the various efforts.

Icebreakers

Because a course on interviewing is concerned with interpersonal interaction and because a desirable approach to teaching the content involves a considerable amount of active participation within the group interaction, you can easily justify beginning with one of the many "icebreaker exercises" available.

The purpose of an icebreaker is to give group members a chance to get acquainted with each other, reduce social distance, increase the level of informality in the group, and help the group develop a sense of cohesion.

Exercise: Introductions

One icebreaker that establishes a pattern for active student participation starts with the instructor asking students to suggest the background data they would like to have about each other—education, work experience, marital status, position in family, and so on. Listing these on the blackboard, students then introduce themselves to each other, covering the suggested items.

You might initiate the icebreaker session by sharing some information about yourself.

Another common icebreaker is to have students introduce themselves individually by stating their principal objective in taking the course and sharing any experience they have in formal interviewing.

A more elaborate procedure is to have the group break up into dyads and interview each other for a total of five minutes about some general biographical information. When the group reconvenes, each member of the dyad introduces the other person to the group based on the dyadic interview.

A more complicated icebreaker is to divide the class into two equal groups and line students up so they are facing each other. The two people facing each other spend two minutes introducing themselves; at that point the lines move one place to the left so that each class member is facing another person. As the class moves, one person at the end of each line will be without a partner. The lone member at the end of one line walks up to meet the lone member at the end of the other line for introduction. The procedure continues until every member of the class has had an opportunity to meet with and be introduced to every other member.

Communication

Exercise: Clarity

One communication problem endemic to human service workers involves habitual use of jargon that makes no sense to the interviewee. Good communication requires that we say what we need to say in a way that the interviewee can understand. The following exercise involves the translation of common social work jargon into the language of the client.

"Translate" the following into English that the average person is likely to understand.

VAGUE PHRASING	CLEAR PHRASING
1. Resistant to authority	_____
2. Negative attitude	_____
3. Developmental Lags	_____
4. Out of touch with reality	_____
5. Flat affect	_____
6. Inability to relate to peers	_____
7. Poor cognitive skills	_____
8. Passive-aggressive personality	_____

Source: Adapted from Robert A. Scott and Peter S. Houts, "Individualized Goal Planning with Families in Social Services," mimeograph, Department of Behavioral Science, College of Medicine, Pennsylvania State University, Hershey, 1978.

Developing Self-Awareness

Developing self-awareness and clarifying values are important requirements for good interviewing. Unless interviewers are explicitly aware of their beliefs in regard to crucial and common human dilemmas, they may not recognize, and hence will be unable to control, the resulting distortion of the direction of the interview.

Exercises that elicit responses to situations involving conflicts in values can help students to clarify their values and stimulate their self-awareness. The examples that follow involve such situations and might be used for a class exercise and class discussion.

A greater level of self-awareness alerts students to those questions that are problematic and areas of sensitivity for them. Without being aware of these considerations they may in fact avoid raising questions about these matters in the interview. They may subconsciously shut off discussion of these areas when the client raises them.

Exercise: Values

For this exercise you can write a description of an incident on the blackboard or a flip chart and solicit reactions from students. Another approach is to photocopy each incident on a separate sheet of paper, leaving room for students to respond in writing. After the students write their responses, the instructor solicits their responses.

1. You are interviewing a 15-year-old girl who tells you she is sexually active and fearful she could become pregnant. She wants your help in getting contraceptive pills but does not want her parents to know about it. What would you do?

2. The client is a 23-year-old woman who gave birth to twins a week ago. She wants help in obtaining day care of some kind for the children, because she is interested in returning to her job as an insurance underwriter. Her husband, who is the owner of a thriving computer software concern, wants her to stay home with the children; the family does not need her income. What would you do?

3. A social worker in a nursing home is asked to help a 79-year-old man and a 78-year-old woman change their room arrangements so that they can room together. They have been visiting each other in their current room setup for the purpose of having sex. They would now like to room together. What would you do?

4. You and your spouse have been having difficulty with your 8-year-old son who is neurotic and having nightmares. He is not doing well in school, and the teacher has suggested that you consult the local mental health center. What would you do?

5. As a worker at a family service agency you have been seeing Roland and Renata Carr for treatment of their marital problems over a period of six months. Recently, Renata Carr has given birth to a son who has a serious congenital anomaly—spina bifida. The child also has a digestive difficulty and needs surgery. Otherwise, it is highly likely that he will die soon. The Carrs, having agreed to let the child die, have refused permission for the operation and have asked you what you think of their decision. What would you say?

6. The client is requesting help in resolving a problem with his significant other, with whom he has been living in an intimate relationship for the past two years. Until recently, they have gotten along well together, and the relationship has been satisfying, emotionally and sexually. Your client, a 25-year-old man, is a homosexual living with another 25-year-old man. Your client has learned that he is HIV positive but does not want to tell his companion for fear of losing him. What would you say?

7. A colleague sees you at a social event and remarks that she knows a friend of hers is seeing you for therapy. She begins to talk about problems she knows your client is experiencing and then asks you whether it is true that the client has been hospitalized previously for depression. What would you say?

8. An African American couple applied and has been approved to adopt. They have been waiting for a child for some time. You have a child available for adoption whose mother was white, the father African American. The child appears to be Caucasian in features and coloration.

A waiting white couple has also been approved for adoption. With which couple would you place the child?

9. The client is a 45-year-old woman who wants help making a decision about her 86-year-old father. Disabled and ill, he has been living in the client's home. He requires considerable attention and care, which the client finds difficult to provide because she has three schoolaged children and her husband works long hours. The client wants to place her father in a nursing home, but he is adamantly opposed to this. What do you think she should do?

10. As a correctional and social worker in a medium-security prison you have developed an effective working relationship with a young inmate who has begun to confide in you. Recently, he told you in confidence he has sharpened a scrap of metal into a knife and plans to cut up an inmate who once assaulted him. He seems serious about this and you have been unable to dissuade him. Would you share this information with the prison authorities?

11. A 17-year-old has requested your help in obtaining an abortion. The pregnancy was accidental and she knew the man only casually. The young woman's parents are staunch Catholics and strongly opposed to abortion. The teenager would not want her parents informed about this. What would you do?

12. Your client is a hyperactive child, Dick, who tends on occasion to disrupt his public school class. The teacher wants him placed in a special class out of consideration for the educational needs of the other twenty-two students. The parents feel that removing Dick from the class will label him, stigmatize him, and deny him a normal peer experience to which he is entitled. What would you do?

13. You are a worker in a protective service unit. In response to a report of child abuse you are visiting a family of immigrants. The mother readily admits that she has used a belt to discipline her 5-year-old son. She says that she is following the teaching of her culture that says, "You have to use corporal punishment if you expect a child to grow up straight." What would you say?

14. As a worker in a mental health clinic you are counseling a client who was referred with a problem of substance abuse. During the course of your interviewing the client reveals that he had sexually molested his 11-year-old daughter. He tells you this after he says, "Everything I tell you is confidential, no?" What would you say?

Exercise: Value Priorities

Students can develop a heightened sense of what they stand for, the values and attitudes they espouse, and the ones they reject by by being required them to select models who represent clearly identified and different points of view. You can set these structured experiences up in a number of different ways. What they have in common is the direction to include some person the student prefers and exclude someone the student rejects.

The instructor gives the student a list of public figures who are known to most of the class and who are generally perceived as clearly representing some point of view. Such lists might include the following:

Pat Schroeder	Rush Limbaugh	Jesse Helms
Jesse Jackson	Robert Redford	George Bush
Al Gore	Gloria Steinem	Thurgood Marshall
Kwesi Mfume	Janet Reno	Barbara Jordan

Make the list as current as possible in regard to point of view of time and geography. The situation students face follows:

All on the list are terminally ill. A new discovery will enable the doctors to cure the disease, but they have only enough serum to cure two or three in the group. The student selects those to whom the medicine should be given.

After making their choices, students should describe in writing the criteria they used to select those they would save. The students use their written statements in participating in the subsequent group discussion of choice criteria.

Exercise: Stereotypes

In making stereotypes explicit the instructor might ask the class to participate in an exercise such as the following:

Write a paragraph on what you anticipate about the behavior, attitudes, and values of an interviewee who is identified by the following:

1. An unmarried, older, white female
2. An adolescent African American male
3. A middle-aged white plumber
4. A young, pregnant, white housewife
5. A white 40-year-old female banker who wears a pinstriped vested suit, tie, well-shined black pumps, and carries a Gucci briefcase.
6. A barely 30-year-old white male, slightly pot-bellied, construction worker just coming off the job so that he is carrying a hard hat; some of the dust of the job is on his overalls, and he smells slightly of stale beer.

Exercise: Interpersonal Preferences

Another approach to developing self-awareness related to the problems of interviewing is to ask students to rate their perception of the difficulty they feel that they might have in interviewing different kinds of clients.

Check the level of difficulty you think you might have in interviewing the following kinds of clients:

Client description	No difficulty	A little difficulty	Moderate difficulty	Very difficult	Extremely difficult
			Level of difficulty		
A highly emotional client	_____	_____	_____	_____	_____
A dependent client	_____	_____	_____	_____	_____
A hostile client	_____	_____	_____	_____	_____
A handicapped client	_____	_____	_____	_____	_____
A very old client	_____	_____	_____	_____	_____
A mentally ill client	_____	_____	_____	_____	_____
A client with a very low IQ	_____	_____	_____	_____	_____
A resistive client	_____	_____	_____	_____	_____
A severely depressed client	_____	_____	_____	_____	_____
A seductive client	_____	_____	_____	_____	_____
A client charged with sexual child abuse	_____	_____	_____	_____	_____
A wife batterer	_____	_____	_____	_____	_____
A terminally ill client	_____	_____	_____	_____	_____

A client who rambles and is unfocused	_____	_____	_____	_____	_____
A preschool child	_____	_____	_____	_____	_____
An adolescent girl	_____	_____	_____	_____	_____
A substance abuser	_____	_____	_____	_____	_____

Exercise: Intrapersonal Preferences

By being forced to make choices about their preferences, students may develop a greater sense of self-awareness. Instructors using this exercise instruct students to check their preference in each of the following pairs:

1. _____ Quiet thoughtful time alone

   _____ Active energetic times with people

2. _____ Being called imaginative or intuitive

   _____ Being called factual and accurate

3. _____ Breaking deadlines

   _____ Setting a schedule and sticking to it

4. _____ Being thought of as a thinking person

   _____ Being thought of as a feeling person

5. _____ Starting meetings at a prearranged time

   _____ Starting meetings when all are comfortable and ready

6. _____ Meeting new people

   _____ Being alone or with one person you know well

Sentence completion items help develop a sense of self-awareness. Complete the following sentence stubs:

I am the kind of person who likes to _____.

Someday I would like to _____.

I am most reluctant to share with others the fact that I am _____.

_____

Two things I am really good at are

1. _____.

2. _____.

One thing about me I would like to change is _____.

If I had two wishes, I would wish for

1. _____.

2. _____.

When I find time to be alone, I most like to _____.

The kind of person I like best is _____.

The two things that most annoy me about some people's behavior are

1. _____.

2. _____.

The feeling with which I have the most trouble is _____.

It hurts me when _____.

One thing I have always wanted to talk more about is_____

_____

The part of my body I like most is _____.

I feel tender toward people when _____.

The thing I value most in life is _____.

When I am approaching an important deadline I _____

_____

I think others see me as _____.

In groups of people whom I have just met, I tend to be _____

_____.

I tend to be rebellious when _____.

I usually react to negative criticism by _____.

I usually hide or camouflage my feelings when _____.

I am most likely to assert myself when _____.

Empathy

Developing a greater degree of conscious self-awareness helps put students in touch with their feelings. Empathy suggests the ability to consciously perceive the feelings of the interviewee and to respond understandingly. The following exercise helps to sensitize students to levels of emphatic responses.

Exercise: Empathic Skills

Read each of the following statements and try to identify in your mind what the speaker felt while making the statement. After you have identified what you think the speaker felt, rate the responses that are already given according to how well each identifies and responds to the person's feelings. Responses that relate to feelings are helpful empathic intervention. On the scale of 1 to 5, 1 means poor or unhelpful and 5 means good or very helpful. A rating of 3 is the midpoint, so to speak, between good and poor responses. Use the following scale to rate the response:

1—Fails to recognize either feelings or content

2—Misses basic feelings but may identify content

3—Identifies and responds to obvious feelings the person is expressing

4—Responds to feelings the person may not be expressing directly

5—Understands underlying feelings, perhaps even better than the person speaking

Statement 1 I've tried and tried and nothing seems right. Now Susan is sick and doesn't seem to be getting any better. She just keeps crying. It seems that all the kids have been sick, but the others got O.K. by themselves. I don't know about Susan. I really don't know what to do about anything anymore.

Use the 5-point scale provided to rate the responses that follow. Circle your rating of these responses.

a.   1   2   3   4   5   You'd better get your baby to a doctor; her problems could be serious.

b.   1   2   3   4   5   You almost seem tired of trying, almost like you would like to just give up.

c.   1   2   3   4   5   I see that you have got problems, but you must be optimistic—don't let life's little trials get you down.

d.   1   2   3   4   5   You're worried about Susan, but you are asking other questions too.

Statement 2   Every day you're here at my doorstep, telling me about something Johnny has done wrong at the center. What do they pay you to do—to come on my doorstep or to work with kids?

Use the 5-point scale provided to rate the responses that follow. Circle your rating of these responses.

a.   1   2   3   4   5   I guess you do get pretty angry with my always reporting about Johnny's problem.

b.   1   2   3   4   5   Well, it seems most of Johnny's problems originate at home and we have to help you with your problems in order to help him.

c.   1   2   3   4   5   You seem like you would like me to just leave you alone and try to work out Johnny's problems at the center.

d.   1   2   3   4   5   I can't help it if you've got a problem child.

Statement 3   I really don't guess you can help me, I don't guess you can. After my husband left, he was supposed to give me sixty dollars a week, but he doesn't give me but ten dollars. I don't have much food for the children, and they've cut off my gas and electricity. He makes a lot of money so I can't get any welfare. The welfare lady said I would just have to get the police to get him. I don't know what to do—I don't want my children going hungry.

Use the 5-point scale provided to rate the responses that follow. Circle your rating of these responses.

a.   1   2   3   4   5   Looks like you have a lot of responsibility, the children and all, but right now you feel almost helpless to do anything about your dilemma.

b.   1   2   3   4   5   You seem like you're at the end of your rope and don't really know what you can do now.

c.   1   2   3   4   5   If you explain your situation to the welfare agency, they will help. Just keep at them until they listen.

d.   1   2   3   4   5   Your husband seems like a bum; you want to call the police from my office?

Exercise: Identifying Empathic Responses

Interviewer–Interviewee

The following presents a series of brief interactions between an interviewee and an interviewer. Mark each interviewer's response according to whether you think the response is empathic or not empathic.

1. INTERVIEWEE: I don't know why the plan is to discharge me from the hospital now. I am still sick and there is no one at home to help me.
   INTERVIEWER: You feel upset and anxious about being forced to leave the hospital now.

   _____empathic   _____not empathic

2. INTERVIEWEE: I have been coming to see you now for four months because the court ordered this counseling. I don't see that it has helped in any way.

   INTERVIEWER: Well, as long as the court ordered it, I guess we will have to continue to meet.

   _____empathic   _____not empathic

3. INTERVIEWEE: Okay, so I drink more than I should. But then, if I lose my license, I can't get to work, so I lose my job, and it just makes things worse.

   INTERVIEWER: You think what they are doing is unfair. It just makes resolving your problems more difficult.

      _____empathic   _____not empathic

4. INTERVIEWEE: So you apply for the job and they find you're an ex-con. Bang. You're outta there. How can you make it?

   INTERVIEWER: Well, didn't you realize that this would be one of the problems you would have to deal with?

      _____empathic   _____not empathic

5. INTERVIEWEE: My mother is like the rest of the family. Nobody makes an effort to understand. Nobody makes an effort to help me in any way.

   INTERVIEWER: You feel abandoned by those you might have thought would be there to help you.

      _____empathic   _____not empathic

Peer Exercise: Empathy

Students in the class are paired. One student in the pair, designated as interviewee, shares some personal details with the interviewer. Interviewers select responses that they think are empathic. Interviewees provide feedback on their perception of how empathic the interviewer is. Interviewees and interviewers change places and repeat the exercise.

Feelings

Recognizing feelings precedes labeling them accurately. Consequently, this exercise should precede the exercise that requires students to identify their feelings accurately. The first exercise involves reading a statement and recognizing the feeling that is likely to accompany the statement. A list of feelings follows each statement. Ask students to select from the list the adjective that best describes the feeling being expressed.

Exercise: Recognizing Feelings

1. STATEMENT: I don't know what to do, I'm just going to have to give up. Nothing I do is right.

FEELINGS: Resignation, futility, hopelessness, depression, discourage-
ment, unhappiness, frustration, desperation

2. STATEMENT: My daughter suddenly told me I could no longer live
with her and her family. I just didn't know what to say,
what to do.

FEELINGS: Surprise, confusion, rejection, hurt, anger, anxiety, shock

3. STATEMENT: You seem to understand what I'm talking about. You have
no idea how hard it is to get people to understand. This is
really great.

FEELINGS: Gratefulness, happiness, acceptance, relief

What are the feelings implicit but not expressed in the following statements?
For the following statements identify in one word the feeling expressed:

1. STATEMENT: My husband just lost his job after working there for eighteen years, and I don't know how we'll keep up with the
payments.

FEELINGS: _____

2. STATEMENT: Tomorrow's Friday, the welcome end of a long week.

FEELINGS: _____

3. STATEMENT: You just learned to drive, so please come home while it's
still light out.

FEELINGS: _____

4. STATEMENT: You never say anything supportive about my career even
though you know how stressful my job is.

FEELINGS: _____

5. STATEMENT: I work harder than he does, but he seems to get all the
breaks.

FEELINGS: _____

To accurately identify feelings we may need a more precise vocabulary
than we ordinarily use. We may need to have available words we can use to
show our understanding of nuances of feeling.

An exercise might help students develop skill in doing this. Ask students
to write *Fear, Happiness, Anger, and Sadness* across the top of the page. These
are general descriptive terms for different but clearly identifiable feelings.
Ask students to write all the words they can think of that express shades of

each feeling. Thus under Anger a student might write *irritation, indignation, rage, exasperation, crossness, ire, peeve, fury, huffiness,* and so on. Class discussion of the individual listings can result in a lengthy list of words that express the many shades of anger.

The richer the vocabulary at interviewers' command, the greater the likelihood that they will be able to select the word that comes closest to expressing their recognition of the feelings of the interviewee.

Exercise: Reflecting Feelings

Identifying feelings precedes reflecting feelings. Students have to be able to accurately identify what the client is feeling before they attempt to reflect feelings. This exercise gives students a series of statements by clients, followed by a choice of responses. The student is asked to selected the best reflected response.

1. I'm just fed up with my father. He's always telling me what to do.
2. The future looks really good; I'm looking forward to it.
3. I can't stand those long lines in the bank.
4. Each time I go to the dentist, I tremble.
5. It's going to be so great—I can't wait to get started.
6. There's no future, so why should I do anything?
7. By the time he does get home, I'm just so concerned.
8. I just lost my job because of those politicians and their economic mismanagement.

The following statements are responses that an interviewer might make in reflecting the feelings expressed by the client in each of the previous statements. Circle the one that you think best reflects the client's feelings.

1. You sound (irritated, angry, hostile).
2. You're really (hopeful, happy, optimistic) about your future.
3. Waiting makes you feel (impatient, fed up, annoyed).
4. You feel (tense, anxious, perturbed) on those occasions.
5. It sounds as though you're full of (enthusiasm, excitement, eagerness).
6. You seem to be (depressed, down, discouraged) right now.
7. In other words, you become (anxious, tense, uptight) when he is delayed.
8. You're really (bitter, resentful, frustrated) about what's happened to you.

Exercise: Identifying and Reflecting Feelings

An exercise that combines identification and reflection of feelings offers students a series of direct statements and asks them to first identify the feeling expressed by the client and then to formulate a statement that reflects the feeling identified.

I. STATEMENT: Things will never be the same. It's terrible. I feel like giving up.

IDENTIFIED FEELINGS: _____

RESPONSE: _____

2. STATEMENT: I never thought I'd feel that way about a son of mine. I've always been so proud of him. I loved him so much and did everything I could to raise him right. Now he goes out and does a thing like this.

IDENTIFIED FEELINGS: _____

RESPONSE: _____

3. STATEMENT: I don't trust my doctor. He says one thing to me and another to my children. I wish I didn't have to go back.

IDENTIFIED FEELINGS: _____

RESPONSE: _____

4. STATEMENT: I'd like to talk about it, but I just can't. It's one of those things we were raised not to talk about. It's just too personal a thing to talk over with someone, especially a stranger.

IDENTIFIED FEELINGS: _____

RESPONSE: _____

5. STATEMENT: Both Jane and Sue showed up at the party in dresses and with dates, and there I was alone and wearing slacks.

IDENTIFIED FEELINGS: _____

RESPONSE: _____

6. STATEMENT: I worked long and hard to help her get through law school and right after she passes the bar exam, she kisses me goodbye.

IDENTIFIED FEELINGS: _____

RESPONSE: _____

Extending the Range and Depth of the Interview

After learning to recognize and identify feelings, students need practice in the appropriate procedures for following and paraphrasing in order to extend the range and depth of the interview.

Exercise: Verbal Following

Distribute a fifteen- to twenty-minute transcription of segment of a social work interview. Focus on the worker's interventions, and initiate a discussion of the verbal following behavior of the interviewer. Such an exercise enables students to analyze verbal following in an interview for which they have no responsibility and with which they identify only vicariously.

Verbal following requires both attentive listening and some ideas regarding selectivity of emphasis to further the purpose of the interview. An exercise focused on verbal following presents students with a series of client statements and asks the student to formulate an appropriate follow-up response.

I. STATEMENT: *[A mother talking about her 4-year-old son]*: The kid never leaves me alone. He follows me from room to room; he clings to me wherever we go. He's like he's attached to me.

FOLLOWING RESPONSE: _____

2. STATEMENT: *[A 70-year-old woman]*: All my friends and relatives have gone away or passed on. I never had any children, so I am all alone. Nobody knows about me or cares about me.

FOLLOWING RESPONSE: _____

3. STATEMENT: *[A 50-year-old man talking about his job]*: I have been in the shop longer than anybody else, but if somebody has to stay late or cover for someone else, they ask me to do it. I get worse treatment than if I was a new hire.

FOLLOWING RESPONSE: _____

4. STATEMENT: *[A 28-year-old man]*: My wife hems me in too much. She wants me to be home all my free time and to go places with her. I don't get much time to do what I want to do alone.

FOLLOWING RESPONSE: _____

5. STATEMENT *[An 18-year-old female]*: My parents hover over me. I think they are afraid that I'll get hooked on drugs or become pregnant or I don't know what.

FOLLOWING RESPONSE: _____

You can make the exercise somewhat more advanced by asking students to supply their rationale for the following responses they formulated.

1. STATEMENT: [*A 28-year-old divorced woman*]: It's so hard to meet men in this town. Singles bars are out for me. Church groups are mostly a bunch of old women. I don't know where to go.

   FOLLOWING RESPONSE: _____

   RATIONALE: _____

2. STATEMENT: [*A 30-year-old woman talking about her husband*]: We just don't communicate. Either he says nothing and is mostly silent, or if he says something, we immediately get into an argument.

   FOLLOWING RESPONSE: _____

   RATIONALE: _____

3. STATEMENT: [*A 23-year-old male college student*]: Since I flunked out of engineering, I have a big problem. I always wanted to be an engineer, and now that I flunked out, I don't know what I want to be, what I want to do.

   FOLLOWING RESPONSE: _____

   RATIONALE: _____

4. STATEMENT: [*A 40-year-old man*]: I really don't like myself the way I am. I am too overweight. I drink too much. I don't have any strong interests or hobbies, and I don't think many people like me.

   FOLLOWING RESPONSE: _____

   RATIONALE: _____

5. STATEMENT: [*A 28-year-old mother*]: The school keeps calling me about my son. He is either playing hooky or is hitting kids and disrupting the class or fighting with the teacher.

   FOLLOWING RESPONSE: _____

   RATIONALE: _____

Exercise: Paraphrasing

Pair students for role-playing dyads, and instruct the designated interviewer to paraphrase the interviewee's statements. The interviewee in turn shares with the interviewer her perception of the correctness and completeness of the interviewer's paraphrase.

Exercise: Making Interpretations

This exercise involves making explicit the inferences that the interviewer might draw from something or some things the interviewee has said. Such inferences lead to interpretations that the interviewer might share with the interviewee. For example:

Mrs. P., 67, is seeing a social worker regarding a problem she is having with her 45-year-old daughter. The recently divorced daughter has lost her job, is not looking for other employment, and has moved in with the interviewee. Mrs. P. says her daughter is irresponsible about money—she's a spendthrift. Mrs. P. is afraid that her daughter will soon exhaust Mrs. P.'s limited funds. The interviewer also learns from Mrs. P. that she was an alcoholic during much of her daughter's childhood and that Mrs. P. sometimes neglected her daughter. The client says that although she knows she can demand that her daughter stick to a limited budget or can take control of her daughter's money as well as her own, she hesitates to do either because she doesn't want to hurt her daughter.

Making an interpretation, the interviewer says, "I wonder if the fact that you treated your daughter badly when she was a child is stopping you from confronting your daughter with her behavior now?"

What are the clues that support the interviewer's interpretation?

CLUES

_____

_____

_____

_____

This exercise involves (1) making inferences from the statements, (2) identifying the clues that support the inferences, (3) formulating an interpretation to communicate to the interviewee:

1. STATEMENT: My children rarely come to see me. They're always too busy. They always seem rushed when I talk to them. I don't understand it. They always saw that I was good to my mother when she got old. Even if there were things to do for the kids, if she needed me, I went to see her and did what she wanted. Why aren't my kids equally concerned about me?

THE INFERENCE: _____

THE CLUES: _____

THE INTERPRETATION: _____

2. STATEMENT: It isn't as though we didn't want to have a child, like my parents keep asking us to do. We keep trying every time Bill comes back from a trip, which he needs to make if he is going to get ahead in the company. And even if he is going to be away for some time, I can't go with him without missing classes here.

THE INFERENCE: _____

THE CLUES: _____

THE INTERPRETATION: _____

3. STATEMENT: He is beginning to look a lot like his father whom we haven't seen since John [age 6] was a baby. And I try to visit him in the foster home, but something always seems to get in the way.

THE INFERENCE: _____

THE CLUES: _____

THE INTERPRETATION: _____

Listening and Silence

Exercise: Listening

Select a client's statement that runs without interruption for one or two paragraphs from a transcribed social work interview. Read the material to the class as though you were the interviewee and members of the class were the interviewers. Following the reading, ask the class to answer a series of questions you have formulated in advance regarding the client's statement. For each of the statements ask the class to answer from among the following:

True—On the basis of what the client said, the statement is definitely true.
False—On the basis of what the client said, the statement is definitely false.
Question mark—The statement may be true or false, but on the basis of the client's statement I cannot be certain.

An easy way to sensitize students to problems in listening is to use the ongoing class situation for an exercise. Present a brief lecture for about five minutes and then stop in midstream and ask students to write down, in as much detail as they can, what you were saying. Ask them to also write what, as far as they can remember, they were thinking about during the five-minute listening period.

Because students are likely to be extremely hesitant to openly acknowledge failure in listening to you, ask class members to compare notes on what it is they heard and leave the room. Return after giving the class several minutes to discuss the notes, and conduct a discussion of the factors associated with failure in listening.

The classic listening exercise is to test students' listening effectiveness through feedback. Break the class into dyads, and ask the members of the pairs to talk with each other about some matter of mutual interest or concern. After each person talks, each has to reflect what he thinks he heard before he can talk. Each then shares his assessment of whether his partner accurately heard what was said.

Because listening takes place at a variety of different levels, instruct students to parrot verbatim what the speaker has said during the first five minutes of dyadic talk. During the second five minutes the listener paraphrases what the speaker said. During the third five minutes the listener reflects the feelings communicated by the speaker.

Read the following paragraph aloud to the class:

You are the pilot flying a four-engine jet from New York City to Los Angeles. There are seventy-two people on board, including nine children, eighteen married couples, and twenty-two businesspeople. The plane has a crew of five. You left New York City at eight A.M. and expect to arrive in Los Angeles at one P.M. What is the pilot's name?

The answer, of course, is in the first sentence if students have been listening carefully.

To demonstrate distortion in listening ask for six or eight volunteers. Ask all but one to step outside the classroom. Relate a short incident to the remaining volunteer and the rest of the class. The remaining volunteer then calls in one volunteer from the hall and relates the story to that person. That student then calls another student from the hall and relates the story in turn. After all students from the hall have heard the story, the last to hear it shares the story so the class can compare that person's version with the original. Differences between the first and last version are the result of failures in listening.

Exercise: Silence

Pair the class into dyads for a brief role-playing session. Instruct the interviewer to maintain a brief period of silence before responding to the interviewee during the early part of the interview and to increase the length of silence for each response as the interview continues. Have the interviewer start with a two-second period of silence and try to increase this to a ten- or fifteen-second period of silence toward the end. Focus the discussion that follows on the interviewer's feelings about maintaining silence and the difficulties in doing so, the interviewee's feeling response to silence, and the effects of silence on interview interaction.

Question Formulation

You can use short role-playing sessions for question formulation exercises. Pair students for role-playing, and instruct the person assigned the role of the interviewer to consistently ask only closed questions. In the post-interview go-round interviewees share their feelings about being asked only closed questions.

Write on the blackboard some of the questions asked in the role-playing, and ask students to rewrite each question as an open-ended question.

Exercise: Rephrasing Closed Questions

The following is a list of closed questions. Ask students to write an open question in place of the closed question. They should try to use a variety of open questions.

1. Aren't your parents helping you?
2. Do you always argue?
3. Do you try to help?
4. Surely you love your husband?
5. Is it true that you want to leave home?
6. Do you enjoy being with that sort of person?
7. You've never married?
8. Have you stopped fighting with your wife?

9. Shouldn't you consider what your family thinks?
10. Do you want to do something about your problems?
11. Do you have any children?
12. Did you ever consider going back to school?
13. Have you thought of staying home with the child rather than going to work?
14. Don't you think a foster home would be better for your child?
15. Do you have any relatives who might help with the care of your mother?

Exercise: Rephrasing "Why" Questions

Ask students to reformulate each of these "why" questions into a different type of question:

1. You know that you might lose your job, so why do you continue to drink?

   REFORMULATION: _____

2. If it creates a conflict in your marriage, why do you buy so many clothes you don't really need?

   REFORMULATION: _____

3. You say you feel guilty about it, so why do you physically abuse the child?

   REFORMULATION: _____

4. You know about AIDs, so why don't you practice safe sex?

   REFORMULATION: _____

5. Why don't you visit Jimmy in the foster home?

   REFORMULATION: _____

Exercise: Probing

From a broad approach to some area of the interview, moving to greater specificity about the problem situation often requires that the interviewer formulate a series of probe questions. Here is an exercise designed to give students practice in developing probing skills:

Read each of the client statements and then formulate two questions that you might ask in following up on the statement:

1. STATEMENT: I keep forgetting or neglecting to take the medicine the doctor prescribed.

Question 1: _____

Question 2: _____

2. STATEMENT: I looked and looked, but I haven't been able to find a job.

Question 1: _____

Question 2: _____

3. STATEMENT: I wouldn't mind going into a nursing home if I could find one I liked.

Question 1: _____

Question 2: _____

4. STATEMENT: Other kids don't treat him right just because he is retarded.

Question 1: _____

Question 2: _____

5. STATEMENT: We're getting to the bottom of what we have, and the only alternative may be welfare.

Question 1: _____

Question 2: _____

Exercise: Making Information More Concrete for Clarification

For each of the following statements formulate a question designed to elicit more information that clarifies the problem:

1. STATEMENT: My husband often abuses me.

   QUESTION: _____

2. STATEMENT: Frank misbehaves whenever I visit.

   QUESTION: _____

3. STATEMENT: Moving to the new city is going to change my life.

   QUESTION: _____

4. STATEMENT: She spends money on stupid things.

   QUESTION: _____

5. STATEMENT: He's taking drugs, I just know it.

   QUESTION: _____

6. STATEMENT: He's not going to get well; he never follows the doctor's orders.

   QUESTION: _____

7. STATEMENT: The therapy didn't accomplish what we hoped it would.

   QUESTION: _____

8. STATEMENT: I know we're going to have to make changes if we plan to stay together.

   QUESTION: _____

9. STATEMENT: I tried time-out as discipline for Jack, but it never stops his fighting with his sister.

   QUESTION: _____

10. STATEMENT: The date with Henry was a bust, a washout.

    QUESTION: _____

11. STATEMENT: I just don't feel comfortable doing that kind of work.

    QUESTION: _____

12. STATEMENT: My wife is giving me a lot of trouble.

    QUESTION: _____

13. STATEMENT: When I visit Jane in the institution, I really feel unwelcome.

    QUESTION: _____

14. STATEMENT: I just know that my husband is growing more distant.

    QUESTION: _____

15. STATEMENT: Since my release from prison I just can't seem to get settled.

    QUESTION: _____

Exercise: Concreteness

An exercise in concreteness requires that students take a series of vague statements and restate them with greater precision.

Explain that the statement, "Most people bore me," might be restated more concretely as "Most people are not very interesting. They talk to me about things that concern them but are of no concern to me. They say what they have to say with a lot of unimportant details and take a long time getting to the point."

Then give students a series of statements, and ask them to elaborate in a similar manner. For example,

1. My husband tends to dominate me.
2. My youngest daughter can be quite annoying.
3. The trip was interesting.
4. We had a productive group meeting.
5. I learned a lot from the last class session.
6. The date last night was a washout.
7. I am a sensitive person.
8. Retirement is going to change my life.
9. My in-laws are the source of a lot of trouble.

Exercise: Concreteness and Immediacy

The following exercise helps develop skills in responding to clients' statements by formulating responses designed to elicit more concrete and immediate information. In this exercise you offer students a client's statement and instruct them to formulate a question that would elicit greater concreteness:

CLIENT STATEMENTS	MODEL RESPONSES SUGGESTED
1. ADOLESCENT [*Speaking of his recent recommitment to a correctional institution*]: It really seems weird to be back here.	1. In what way does it seem weird?
2. CLIENT: You can't depend on friends; they'll stab you in the back every time.	2. I gather you feel that your friends have let you down in the past. Could you give me a recent example in which this has happened?
3. CLIENT: He's got a terrible tem-	3. Could you tell me more about

per—that's the way he is, and he'll never change.

what happens when he loses his temper with you? or You sound like you don't have much hope that he'll ever get control of his temper. What makes you think that he will never change? (You might explore each aspect of the message separately.)

4. CLIENT: My supervisor is so insensitive, you can't believe it. All she thinks about is reports and deadlines.

4. Could you give me some examples of how she is insensitive to you?

5. CLIENT: My dad's fifty-eight years old now, but I swear he still hasn't grown up. He has a chip on his shoulder all the time.

5. That must make it difficult for you. Could you recall some recent examples of times you've had difficulties with him?

6. CLIENT: I just have this uneasy feeling about going to the doctor. I guess I've really got a hang-up about it.

6. Think of going to the doctor just now. Let your feelings flow naturally. [*Pause.*] What goes on inside you—your thoughts and feelings?

7. AFRICAN AMERICAN STUDENT [*To African American practitioner*]: You ask why I don't talk to my teacher about why I'm late for school. I'll tell you why. She's got it in for us blacks, and there's just no point talking to her. That's just the way it is.

7. So you see it as pretty hopeless. You feel pretty strong about Ms. Wright. I'd be interested in hearing what's happened that you've come to the conclusion she's got it in for blacks.

8. FATHER: You work and sacrifice for your kids, and what do you get back in return? I'll tell you what you get—just a smart mouth with a lot of demands.

8. That must be very hurtful for you—to feel so unappreciated, taken for granted, and—well— just used by them. I'd like to get a picture of exactly what happens between you and the children. Could you give me some recent examples of times you've experienced those feelings?

9. CLIENT: I'm wondering if you're a student trainee because, if you

9. I gather you want to be sure you're in good hands. Specifi-

are, I'm not sure that you can help me. I think it would take someone with a lot of experience to know what to do in my case.

cally, what do you think I might not be able to understand?

10. SPOKESMAN [*for group to group leader*]: We've been talking about Todd [*absent member*] while you've been gone, and we've decided that we don't want him in the group anymore—he's too flaky.

10. LEADER: I'd be interested in hearing in what way you think Todd is "flaky" and how it has affected the group.

Source: Adapted from Dean Hepworth and Jo Ann Larson, *Direct Social Work Practice: Theory and Skills* (Homewood, Ill.: Dorsey Press, 1982), pp. 134–35.

Exercise: Confrontation

For practicing formulation of confrontation responses, offer students a series of client statements that contain some discrepancy, such as an inconsistency between the interviewee's verbalization and feelings, a client's description of his behavior and the actual behavior, and a client's perception of the situation and the normative perception of the situation. Then ask students to formulate a response that confronts the client with the discrepancy:

1. CLIENT: So what if my wife left me? She's not the only pebble on the beach. Good riddance to bad rubbish [*said in a low monotone, head down, avoiding eye contact*].

   CONFRONTATION: _____

2. CLIENT: Sure I grabbed the gold chain. Look, women shouldn't wear those things. They are just asking to get mugged. It's like an invitation to do it.

   CONFRONTATION: _____

3. CLIENT: Sure I want to get a job. I go down to the employment agency at least once a week and even look at the want ads in the paper sometimes.

   CONFRONTATION: _____

4. CLIENT: I do consider myself a caring mother. I hit her because I care about how she's going to turn out.

   CONFRONTATION: _____

5. CLIENT: [*Smells strongly of alcohol and has difficulty enunciating*]: Sure I want to get off the booze. It's ruining my job, my marriage, and my health.

CONFRONTATION: _____

Overview

Many exercises presented thus far have focused explicitly on some particular kinds of responses in interviewing—reflecting, following, immediacy, and confrontation. The next series of exercises is concerned with more general kinds of responses and is designed to stimulate discussion of the rationale for defining more or less desirable responses. In these exercises the instructor presents a vignette and students formulate or select a response. Then ask students what prompted their selection of one response and the rejection of others. The exercise permits the class to review many basic precepts of interviewing.

Another form of the exercise presents students with a situation, followed by a number of alternatives. Ask students to select the most desirable response. This exercise requires students to recognize a desirable response, whereas the first form of the exercise requires them to formulate a response.

Exercise: Recognizing and Selecting Desirable Interview Responses

Instructions: This is not a test. Imagine that someone has come to you for assistance. Each item represents potential interchanges between you and your client, the person seeking your help. The client begins the conversation by talking about an aspect of the situation she faces. No further information is available on the case. You will not know at what point in the conversation the interchange takes place. In short, you are dealing with an isolated statement. This is followed by five responses that you might make. Using the separate answer sheet, arrange these responses in the order of your preference. Rank each response, using 1 for most desirable and 5 for least desirable.

The wording used may not strike you as being the best, but disregard this factor so long as the response is the type you would favor. You may think of responses that you think would be better than any of the five options, but you must rank the alternatives presented in the order of their desirability.

1. FEMALE [*Age 47*]: I really don't know what to do. Ah—I really don't know whether to go back to teaching school. It gets on my nerves so—I can't hardly stand it. I've got a good salary. Or else make a clean break and really do the thing I'm interested in. [*Slight pause.*] But that would mean

starting in at the bottom with a very small salary, and I wouldn't know whether I could do that or not.

    a. Could you tell me a little more about your new field of interest? It is quite important that we think about this clearly.

    b. Well, before you jump into something new, you should be very sure that it is really worthwhile and will provide at least the security and feeling of contribution that teaching brings you.

    c. Well, now, I may be able to help you with that decision. Probably, you could take some tests that will furnish you with some idea as to whether you might expect to be successful in the line of your new interests. And maybe we could explore some of the things that give you dissatisfaction in your teaching work.

    d. This indecision of yours is an understandable thing and stems from the conflict between your uncertainty over the new line of interest and your mixed feelings of dissatisfaction with the teaching job yet hesitance to leave the security it affords.

    e. It's really a tough decision, isn't it? Whether to take the risks of starting out in a new field or to stick by the security of the irritating teaching job.

2. FEMALE [*Age 19*]: I tell you I hate my father. I hate him! I hate him! I hate him! And there's no reason for it. He is a minister—a good and righteous man. He has never laid a hand on me, but I have this terrific feeling against him. And it makes me feel so terrible because—there's no reason for it. It's a sin to hate your father, especially if you don't have any reason for it. I— It worries me.

    a. Of course you feel guilty about hating him so, especially since you can't put your finger on what he has done to make you hate him. And then too, even though you see only your hatred of him, you'll find that underneath it all you have some love for him, and this plays a part in your feelings of guilt.

    b. I guess everyone at some time or another goes through a period when they hate one or both of their parents. It's really not at all uncommon. Most people find that they can work out some way of getting along until things settle down.

    c. This is certainly something you will want to get cleared up. Happy relationships with parents are too constructive a thing to a person, not only at your age but in the future as well; you won't want to jeopardize what it can mean to you.

    d. It worries you that you should hate your father without reason and yet feel sinful for hating him.

    e. I think we ought to get to the root of that worry. Tell me about your father—all about him. You say he's never laid a hand on you, but maybe he has *not* let you do a number of things *you* wanted to do. Can you think of anything along that line?

3. MALE [*Age 59*]: I couldn't let my son help me now that I'm down and out. I've got that shred of pride left. Because, you see, I remember when he was a kid, I didn't turn my hand to help him. I traipsed around the country. His mother died when the kid was born—and I let the relatives push him around and stuck him in foster homes, and now—it certainly was like a knife stuck in me when we met the other day and he said, "We can make a go of it together, Dad, I've got a little money saved up." No. No, I won't let him do it. I will clear out of here. It'll be hard, but—I haven't done *one* thing for him—or anyone else, for that matter.

    a. Have you investigated the possibility of an old-age pension? Perhaps something could be worked out there that wouldn't make it necessary for you to impose on your son or accept help from him.

    b. What was your married life like? Had you and your wife planned for a child?

    c. Your behavior in the past makes you unworthy of help your son wants to give you now; is that what you mean?

    d. Have you thought about what it will mean to your son if you don't let him do this thing that he wants to do for you?

    e. I see what you mean. You feel that you don't deserve the help he wants to give because in the past you did nothing to earn it. And your statement that you never have done anything for anyone else makes it look as if it might be a real problem to you, to accept responsibility *for* helping others and to accept help from others.

4. FEMALE [*Age 30*]: I've lived in this town for ten years now, and in the same apartment for seven years but I don't know anybody. At the office I just can't seem to make friends. I just freeze up. I try to be nice to the other workers, but I feel all stiff and uncomfortable inside. And then I tell myself that I don't care. People aren't dependable. Everyone is out for himself. I don't want any friends. And sometimes I think I really mean that.

    a. Well, I'll tell you what you can do. You can join a small social group at the Y. Quite a few people go there who have difficulty in making friends. Most want to start out by taking ceramics, leather tooling, or some other handicraft. This gives them something to do as a basis and permits them to make friends slowly and at their own pace. How does that sound to you?

b. Perhaps if you could tell me a little more about how you go about trying to make friends, we could get a clearer idea of what is involved.

c. It's gone on so long it almost has you convinced—is that what you mean?

d. Maybe your not wanting friends is just to protect you from something else.

e. There are a number of things that you might do to learn how to make friends, and the sooner you start the better.

5. MALE [*Age 42*]: But can't you tell me what to do? Can't you make a few suggestions? I'm willing to do *anything*, but I just don't know which way to turn. I'll work *hard* to help myself, if you'll just tell me whether you think it will help me or not. And whether you think I can get over this personality problem. If you'll just tell me what to do, I'll be so grateful to you.

a. Maybe an important part of your situation is that you don't have real confidence in yourself.

b. Really, it's not so important what you do so long as what you do is a product of your self-reliance. You've got to learn to do the things that are good and right because *you* feel they are, not *me*.

c. I gather you just don't feel capable of working this out yourself.

d. Before I could answer any of your questions satisfactorily, I'd have to have quite a bit of information about you, your family, your childhood, your work, your relationships, and your wife and so forth.

e. Well, you've really asked for a lot there, all right. I think I can best answer you in this way: We'll work together talking over these things that bother you. You'll think of some things, and I'll think of some things that maybe you've missed. And maybe between the two of us we'll get to the bottom of all this and figure out a path for you to follow that will solve most, if not all, the problems. I wouldn't worry too much about it. I think we can be fairly sure of making headway.

6. MALE VETERAN [*Age 30*]: What's the use of anything? No one plays fair and square with a guy. The fellows who stayed at home got all the plums. They all took advantage of us while we sweated it out at the front. I hate their guts—every one of them. They are all double-crossers. And my wife . . .

    a. You started to say something about your wife?

    b. You feel they took advantage of you, and it really makes you boil.

    c. You get angry when you see people trying to take advantage of you.

    d. I understand how you feel about that, but it's going to block you from getting ahead if you don't try to get away from it.

    e. You've got lots of company with your anger. It's justifiable in so many cases.

7. MALE [*Age 33*]: I tell you, I am in one hell of a fix. I'm in love with the greatest girl on the face of the earth, and she loves me. I'm sure of that. But I'm not worthy of her. I can't ask her to marry. I've got a criminal record. She doesn't know about that. But I know it'll come out some day. No, I couldn't marry and have children. I've got a record that proves to the world that I'm a first-class s.o.b.

    a. Well, it would certainly be unfair to her to marry and to discover about your past later. Don't you almost have to tell her about it now?

    b. You feel afraid to face her with your record because she might turn you down, and you just couldn't stand that.

    c. Could you tell me a little as to why you're so sure that she wouldn't be able to accept you if she knew about your past?

    d. Perhaps if you were to have her come in to see me, I could talk with her and lead her to see that your past is your past and does not necessarily mean that you couldn't have a happy future together.

    e. You see yourself as unworthy of her beyond all shadow of a doubt.

8. FEMALE [*Age 23 and physically disabled*]: I can't do any of the things my sister does. I can't dance or go riding or date the boys. I'm a—I look at Charlene, and I wish I was her. You can't know the feeling I get deep inside me. I want to be able to have pretty clothes like hers and to go out and have a good time. It makes me sick inside me. But she can't help it. She was born that way. And I can't help it because I was born this way— and I get this feeling. I *love* my sister. Really I do—but I just cried and cried—until I was sick. I want the things other women have. I can't help it. I'm only human. I know it's a sin to feel as I do. But she has *everything* and I have nothing.

    a. Since you aren't going to be able to engage in physical activities as your sister does, I'm wondering if there aren't some other sources of activities that might be satisfying.

b. I can appreciate why you'd envy her so, but since you can't compete with her, it's not much use in using up your energies with envy. You've got to buckle down and build a world that satisfies you.

c. In other words, you feel envious of your sister because you can't compete with her, and you feel guilty about your envy because you love your sister too.

d. I'd like to get a better idea of just how you react to her directly and how she reacts to you in some of these situations.

e. You say in one breath that you envy your sister. You say next that you love her. Now couldn't your feelings of guilt be due to these conflicting feelings?

9. FEMALE [*Age 43*]: I've decided that this is not going to help me. All it does is make me realize what I have to do, and I'm sick of taking responsibility. I don't think I'll come back any more.

a. Of course it has to be your decision. I can't force you to come. But you certainly aren't going to settle anything by backing away from it.

b. This has been too painful to you, and now you want to escape the situation that produces the pain.

c. It just doesn't seem to fill the bill for you.

d. I'd like to know what your thinking has been in coming to this decision.

e. Sometimes taking responsibility can be a pretty demanding thing. Perhaps if you decided to continue coming, we could reach a point where you enjoyed responsibility.

10. MALE [*Age 39*]: There is no other way to handle this than to destroy them completely. Remember, this man was supposed to be my best friend, and he took my wife away from me. And after the divorce he married her. And then he pushed me out of the business. But I've got the evidence to ruin him. I could clean him out and put him behind bars for the rest of his life. [*Laughs bitterly.*] Wouldn't that be something? My ex-wife married to something kept behind bars and not a dime to live on?

a. Your desire to destroy them seems to me to be largely a desire for revenge. It may have grown out of the rejection and denial you experienced from both of them.

b. Wanting to get even is understandable, but don't you think that is going pretty far? I certainly wouldn't do anything I'd regret later.

   c. You want them to suffer at your hand just as they made you suffer at theirs.

   d. After all that, I can see where it would be really satisfying to see them suffer.

   e. Has anyone else ever crossed you like that—in business, among your friends, when you were a kid in school?

Source: Adapted from the *Annual Handbook for Group Facilitators, 1973*.

Cross-Cultural Interviewing

Exercise: Sensitivity to One's Own Ethnic Origins

On the supposition that many in the class, if not most, are members of an ethnic community, this exercise is designed to sensitize students to their ethnic origins. The exercise requires that students write a short paper on their perception of their ethnicity—the national origin of parents or grandparents; the motives that prompted them to come to the United States; the problems they encountered in coming here and getting settled; the residuals of ethnic origins in family diet, language, customs, values, furniture, pictures, family stories and memories; contact with or knowledge of family in the old country; and current contact with ethnic organizations in the United States. The point of the exercise is to get students to think in ethnic terms and become aware of ethnic factors in people's lives.

Nonverbal Communication

General Exercises

The following is a beginning exercise in getting students to identify the meaning they ascribe to some common nonverbal behaviors. Ask students to select from column B the feeling they think is associated with the client behavior described in column A.

COLUMN A	COLUMN B
Nonverbal Communication	What Client May Be Feeling
_____ 1. Client sits very straight and rigidly in his chair. He does not look at you directly. His lips are tight, and when he speaks it is in a high-pitched voice. He speaks rapidly.	a. Anxious b. Happy c. Relaxed

_____ 2. Client takes a comfortable position in a chair. d. Shy
Her facial muscles are relaxed, and she looks
directly at you. Her voice is loud enough for you e. Satisfied
to hear. She speaks at a rate that seems natural
for her. f. Afraid

_____ 3. Client taps his foot. He looks away from g. Angry
you often. He rises and paces during the
session. h. Embarrassed

_____ 4. Client sighs. i. Sad

_____ 5. Client looks sleepy, listless. j. Depressed

_____ 6. Client slouches in a chair. He doesn't appear k. Tense
to hear much of what you say. He looks drawn
and tired. l. Defensive

_____ 7. Client seems silly. She laughs at inappropriate m. Uncomfortable
times.
n. Comfortable

_____ 8. Client talks very softly, choosing words with
extraordinary care. He avoids eye contact and o. Uptight
says little.
p. Scared

_____ 9. Client's face is tightly drawn, and her lips are
pursed. She seems to be glaring at you. Her face q. Annoyed
is slightly flushed.
r. Relieved

_____10. Client's eyes are teary.

_____11. Client misses quite a few sessions. The reasons
he gives for missing sessions seem trivial. When
he arrives, he's late.

_____12. Client always arrives one hour before a
session. There are no apparent transportation
problems.

Recording on the blackboard students' various responses to each behavior is a good illustration of how the same behavior can be interpreted in a variety of ways.

A more advanced format is to ask each student to identify in writing what the following nonverbal behaviors mean:

1. A man walks into your office, takes off his coat, loosens his tie, sits down, and puts his feet up on a chair.
2. A man walks into your office, sits with a straight back, and clasps his arms across his chest before saying a word.
3. Your client rests her cheek on her hand, strokes her chin, cocks her head slightly to one side, and nods deeply.
4. A woman walks into your office, sits as far away as she can, folds her arms, crosses her legs, tilts the chair backward, and looks over your head.
5. A client refuses to talk and avoids eye contact with you.
6. A client gazes at you and stretches out her hands with the palms up.
7. A client quickly covers his mouth with his hand after revealing some sensitive material.
8. You are talking to someone who clenches her hand tightly while using the other hand to grip her wrist or arm.
9. A woman in your office crosses her legs and moves her foot in a slight kicking motion while drumming her fingers.
10. A person sits forward in his chair, tilting his head and nodding at intervals.

Follow this exercise with a class discussion comparing individuals' answers.

Source: Adapted from Barbara Okun, *Effective Helping: Interviewing and Counseling Techniques*, 2d ed. (Monterey, Calif.: Brooks-Cole, 1982), p. 48.

Exercise: Sight Without Sound

The first exercise simulates content discussions about communication and latent versus manifest content in interviews. Ask for two volunteers from the group, and send the others off for a fifteen- to twenty-minute break. While the rest of the group is gone, videotape a ten-minute interview involving a plausible case situation, either from students' experience or drawn from other case examples. Reconvene the group, and watch the videotape *without the sound track* (merely turn the volume down so far that no one can hear it). Instruct the participants to learn what they can from the video portion only. They should have no information about the interview, not even which person is the client and which is the worker. After they watch the tape, ask the participants what they learned about the interview situation. Jot down on the blackboard their speculations or hunches about who is playing the worker, who is playing the client, problem areas, emotional states, interviewing techniques, ego defenses, and so on. Then play the tape back a second time with the sound, and check the accuracy of the class's assumptions.

For the second exercise have different students use the same phrase but with different vocal inflections and facial expressions to illustrate the importance of congruence between verbal and nonverbal behavior. Ask different students to say, "How can I be of help to you today?" with a smile or a frown or a bored expression.

In the third exercise ask students to list nonverbal behaviors that they believe they display when they are feeling some strong feelings—anger, joy, happiness, sadness, and the like. For instance, one student might list the following:

When I am mad, I frown, clench my fists, pull my body up tight, pull away from people, tense up.

When I am sad, I tear up.

Exercise: Self-Identification of Nonverbal Behavior

Here is another exercise designed to help students identify their nonverbal behavior. Identifying and describing nonverbal behavior associated with certain feelings helps people identify more accurately the feelings that others might be experiencing when they see only the nonverbal manifestations.

In the space provided, describe what your bodily appearance might be under the following circumstances:

1. You are at a party where someone is talking incessantly. You find him boring and obtrusive but feel you cannot leave.

   APPEARANCE: _____

2. You are spending an afternoon visiting a favorite friend. You are sitting in your friend's living room or den and enjoying yourself immensely.

   APPEARANCE: _____

3. You are in the presence of an angry person. This person is yelling at you and blaming you for something. You feel the accusations are unjust. The person will not listen to what you have to say.

   APPEARANCE: _____

4. Recall a time when you felt out of place, shy, or inadequate. Imagine yourself in that situation again.

   APPEARANCE: _____

5. You have just told a joke that includes a four-letter word. Nobody laughs, and there is a dead silence in the group. You feel terribly embarrassed.

APPEARANCE: _____

The game Charades depends of course on transmitting and decoding nonverbal behaviors. You can adapt Charades to the social work context. Assign a student to play an involuntary client coming to an agency. The class has to identify the student as an involuntary client.

Still another exercise assigns a student to play a client who has just suffered a grievous loss—death of a child or a spouse, for example. The class has to identify the principal affect communicated.

Exercise: Vocal Cues

Telephone Interview This exercise requires an attempt to simulate a telephone interview, which of course is how many social workers conduct some of their client contacts. It is important to eliminate all visual contact. This can be done by having participants interview each other with a blackboard or screen between them or to have participants actually talk to each other over the phone from different parts of the building with other class members observing them at each end. Another possibility is to have participants sit with their backs to each other and conduct an interview as if they were on the phone. Telephone contacts permit communication of vocal cues but no body, facial, or eye gestures, thus limiting the amount of nonverbal information.

Vocal Aspects Conduct the class as usual, except that you hold the discussion in total darkness, if you are in a room that permits this, or ask students to agree to be blindfolded. The object of the exercise is to have students focus as sharply as possible on vocal components of nonverbal communication.

The postexercise discussion centers on students' picking up on the changes in volume, speed, pitch, inflection, cadence, and so on that they noted in listening to the class discussion while in the dark or blindfolded.

Exercise: Proxemics

Divide the class into two groups, pairing students from each group to talk about some questions of general interest. Draw one group aside and tell these students that during the conversation they should progressively reduce the physical distance between them and their partners, one inch or so every few minutes. The informed member of the dyad thus attempts to intrude on the personal space of the uninformed conversational partner. The exercise demonstrates the response to proxemic nonverbal behavior.

Exercise: Partializing and Systematizing Observations

Because nonverbal behavior is multifaceted, the instructor may need to *partialize student observation.*

Assign a pair of students to role-play in front of the group. Then assign other students to monitor different aspects of nonverbal communication: two students to monitor eye contact; two students to monitor facial gestures (including smiling); two students to monitor vocal inflections and vocal changes in volume, pace, and emphasis; two students to monitor changes in body position; two students to observe hand and arm gestures. The goal of the discussion that follows is the totality of a communication as reflected in its parts and as those parts relate to the interview content.

In sensitizing students to a greater awareness of nonverbal communication, it helps to organize their observations systematically. You might devise a handout such as the following, give it to students, and ask them to observe the client's nonverbal behavior as displayed in a role-playing session, a movie, or a videotape presented to the class.

1. How does the client sit?

   a. _____ Rigidly _____ relaxed _____ slouched

   b. _____ Near the counselor _____ at a normal distance
   _____ far away

   c. _____ Fairly upright _____ leaning forward
   _____ leaning backward

   d. _____ Moving constantly _____ moving appropriately
   _____ never moving

   e. _____ Looking at counselor _____ sometimes looking at
   counselor _____ never looking at counselor

2. How does the client speak?

   a. _____ Too quickly _____ at a normal pace _____ slowly
   _____ very slowly

b. _____ Very loudly _____ in a normal tone _____ softly

_____ barely audibly

c. _____ With excess emotion _____ with some emotion

_____ with no emotion

d. _____ With many gestures _____ with some gestures

_____ with no gestures

e. _____ With appropriate affect _____ with inappropriate affect

_____ with no affect

3. How does the client look?

a. _____ Coloring intense _____ coloring normal _____ pale

and wan

b. _____ Happy _____ normal _____ sad _____ teary

c. _____ Well-dressed _____ normally dressed _____ disheveled

d. _____ Very overweight _____ normal weight _____ very thin

e. _____ Friendly _____ businesslike _____ belligerent

_____ meek

Exercise: Artifactual Communication

On behalf of a client you have scheduled an interview with the personnel manager of a large manufacturing concern. Your client has applied for a job with the organization, and you are his advocate. In addition, you hope to learn whether the company has additional openings that might be appropriate for other clients.

The personnel manager has been unavoidably detained and will be back in the office in about fifteen minutes. The receptionist asks you to wait in the personnel manager's office. As you examine the office carefully for clues to who the personnel manager is, you observe the following:

The large desk is off to the side of the room and faces a large window that overlooks the factory parking lot.

The manager's tilt-back chair faces the window, and the interviewee's straight-back chair is across the desk, facing the manager's chair.

The manager's chair is leather covered, as is the desk top.

The desk top is clear of all papers, and correspondence is neatly piled in in and out baskets to the side.

A book of matches from a local expensive supper club is on the desk. To one side are a desk calendar, stapler, and tape dispenser.

A picture holder has snapshots of two children on one side, a boy about 6 and a girl about 3. On the other side of the picture holder is a picture of a woman in her late twenties, with close-cropped hair, dangling earrings, and harlequin glasses.

The floor is covered with a sea-green rug.

The walls are painted a bluish gray and hold a series of pictures of sailboat and marine landscapes.

A cactus plant occupies one corner.

Away from the desk a small table holds a dictionary, *Roget's Thesaurus*, several magazines (*Time, Readers Digest, Sports Illustrated*), and a folded copy of the *Wall Street Journal*.

Against a third wall is a glass-enclosed bookcase. You note books on personnel management, organizational psychology, and counseling.

Use your observations of the room's contents, arrangements, and decor to write a short description of the personnel manager whom you will be meeting shortly.

You might want to use this exercise merely as an example and formulate a similar descriptive vignette for a social work interviewing room as viewed by the client. Or perhaps the living room or kitchen in a client's home where a home visit is scheduled.

Check the layout of your classroom. What messages do you think its furnishing and arrangements—the lighting, decor, and such—communicate?

You might consider coming to class dressed in a manner that is atypical for a professor. After class ask students how they reacted to seeing a professor dressed in this manner.

Interview Assessment

In asking students to evaluate an interview they have observed —a role-playing session, an audiotape, a videotape, or a movie— it might be best to provide a structured guide to critiquing an interview. Included here is variety of critique guides tailored to the different formats that may be used for this purpose.

Exercise: Checklist of What to Look for in Evaluating an Interview

1. Good question formulation
   a. Rarely suggests answers to questions.
   b. Clearly and precisely phrases questions
   c. Asks only one question at a time.
   d. Formulations rarely call for only yes or no,—in other words, usually are open ended.
   e. Tactfully phrases questions.
   f. Questions are brief and to the point.
   g. Questions are well timed.
   h. Frame of reference for questions is clear.
   i. Question is a response to client's need rather than worker's needs.
2. Maintains interview structure; when client rambles, does not permit unproductive, prolonged, irrelevant digression.
3. Structure offers client freedom to introduce material that may be pertinent.
4. Smooth rather than abrupt transitions.
5. Rarely interrupts or overrides client.
6. Rarely keeps talking for the client, finishes client's sentences, or puts words in client's mouth.
7. Does not break silence prematurely but also does not permit a silence that is too long.
8. Gives summaries or offers recapitulations where appropriate.
9. Appropriate interviewer role performance
   a. Rarely uses highly personal references
   b. Never makes unprofessional statements
   c. Rarely permits prolonged small talked.
   d. Rarely abdicates control of interview
10. Responses are human and concerned, seem spontaneous; appropriate use of feeling statements.
11. Attempts at exploration are comfortable, effective, show assurance.
12. Interpretation well timed or appropriate in view of manifest and latent content of client's preceding statement.
13. Intervention clearly relevant to purpose of interview.
14. Choice of language and wording appropriate for the client.
15. Takes steps to help client with some difficulty in communication.
16. Good use of probes when interview calls for it.

17. Uses praise frequently and appropriately.
18. Affect is consistent with words.
19. Physical gestures indicate interest, attention, concern.
20. Attentive, alert manner of listening.
21. Does not take over client's problem, giving advice inappropriately.
22. Expression of both positive and negative feelings accepted.
23. Gives support and encouragement appropriately.
24. Evidences a respectful accepting attitude toward interviewee.
25. Clearly makes efforts to be empathically understanding.

Exercise: Criteria for Evaluating Initial Interviewing Skills

	Poor	Fair	Good	Excellent
1. Putting client at ease	——	——	——	——
2. Attending behaviors: relaxed posture, eye contact, verbal following	——	——	——	——
3. Selective attending	——	——	——	——
4. Minimal encouragement	——	——	——	——
5. Open invitation to talk	——	——	——	——
6. Goal setting/clarifying	——	——	——	——
7. Information giving	——	——	——	——
8. Information seeking	——	——	——	——
9. Questioning skills— probing, open ended	——	——	——	——
10. Seeking concreteness	——	——	——	——
11. Clarification	——	——	——	——
12. Note taking	——	——	——	——
13. Reflection	——	——	——	——

Potential Mistakes

1. Premature confrontation

(advice giving) —— —— —— ——

3. Talking too much   _____   _____   _____   _____

4. Too many questions   _____   _____   _____   _____

5. Garbled questions   _____   _____   _____   _____

6. Double questions   _____   _____   _____   _____

7. Interrupting   _____   _____   _____   _____

Exercise: Interview Evaluation Scale

This scale is graded from 1 (poor) to 5 (excellent) for evaluating the interviewer in terms of level of performance for each item.

INITIAL INTERVIEW

5. Warm salutation. Gives client positive acceptance and welcome. Explains purpose of interview.
4. Warm greeting. Explains procedure but not purpose.
3. Greeting—tone, expression acceptable.
2. Brief recognition, with no attempt to put interviewee at ease.
1. Makes no attempt made to set up the interview.

FACE OF INTERVIEWER

5. Definitely comfortable, not smug but confident.
4. Comfortable, well-controlled manner.
3. No obvious discomfort—apparently at ease.
2. Moderate discomfort—some tension, anxiety, and such noted.
1. Much discomfort—definitely hesitation at interview.

EASE OF INTERVIEWEE

5. Quite at ease, comfortable, confident.
4. Easy, forthright manner.
3. No obvious discomfort—apparently at ease.
2. Some discomfort, lack of confidence, anxiety, hesitance, hostility.
1. Much discomfort, ill at ease, loss of self-control.

CONTROL OF INTERVIEW

5. Interviewer is courteous, capable leader. Demonstrates ability to direct interview effectively.
4. Interviewer recognizes and maintains role.
3. Interviewer is in charge throughout but without positive effectiveness.

2. Interviewer partially loses control or somewhat overcontrols.
1. Interviewer loses control to point of ineffectiveness or rigid overcontrol.

PERTINENCE

5. Superior skill and expertise in questions and comments.
4. Demonstrates skill in eliciting adequate responses.
3. Questions and comments get adequate response.
2. Inappropriate questioning.
1. Misleading, faulty questioning.

TRANSITION

5. Logical, positive transitions that follow client from clue to clue without sticking rigidly to a pattern.
4. Orderly transition except for occasional diversion.
3. No evidence of order but not haphazard or slap-dash.
2. Haphazard, thoughtless, careless.
1. Obviously confusing to interviewee.

TERMINATION

5. Interviewer takes full responsibility and clarifies next move.
4. Interviewer puts interviewee at case about what happens next.
3. Interviewer makes some reasonable attempt to set up interviewee's next move.
2. Interviewer takes little or no responsibility to set up next move.
1. Interviewer avoids definite challenge from interviewee as to what happens next.

Source: Adapted from A. J. Backrach and E. G. Pattishall, "A Method of Evaluating Student Interviewing," *Journal of Medical Education* 32 (1957):853.

Further Suggestions

Semester Assignments

The ultimate test of what students have learned in the course is an actual interview that each student conducts, tapes, transcribes, and analyzes. The task is outlined in the suggested semester assignment that follows.

Assignment: Conducting and Analyzing a Social Work Interview

Instructions for the Student

Step 1: Getting the interview Tape record an interview in which you are the interviewer. If you are working in an agency or have a fieldwork place ment that provides you an opportunity to interview a client, this would be preferable. If such an interview is not possible, try to arrange to interview a friend, neighbor, or classmate about some problem, concern, or event of mutual interest. In every instance obtain the interviewee's permission to record and, in the case of an agency interview, obtain the permission of your supervisor as well.

The interview should last as long as it takes to achieve the particular purpose of the interview. If this means an interview of twenty minutes, the length of the interview is twenty minutes; if this means an hour and twenty minutes, the length of the interview is an hour and twenty minutes. We would hope to get from you an interview long enough to show, with some sufficiency and detail, your interviewing skills.

For the reader to have some idea of the context in which the interview was conducted, please include on a *separate* page *before* the interview typescript itself a *short* paragraph containing the following information: the kind of agency in which the interview was conducted; if available, the age, sex, socioeconomic level, and occupation of the person interviewed; the general problems that prompted the contact between client and agency; the number of previous contacts, if any, with the client; and the general purpose of the interview conducted.

Step 2: Transcribing the tape After taping the interview, transcribe it or have it transcribed. Please double space.

In transcribing the tape use parentheses to state the significant nonverbal interaction. Thus if the tape reflects a pause of three to six seconds, note in parentheses (short pause). If you have a pause of seven seconds or longer, note in parentheses (long pause). If there is laughter at any point, note this in parentheses; if the client cries, note this in parentheses; if there is a sharp intake of breath or long sigh or noticeably increased vehemence in what the client is saying, note this in parentheses. We are trying to get into the typescript any affect that appears on the tape but does not appear as words uttered.

Number each comment. Thus your first question or comment would be w1 (worker 1). The client's first response would be c1 (CLIENT 1). The next time you say something, number it w2 (WORKER 2) and so on.

Step 3: Retrospective/introspective comments After the tape is transcribed, read the transcription and/or listen to the tape.

Analyze retrospectively the response you experienced at each point in the interview and the thinking that prompted you to say what you said and do what you did. This is a process of retrospective introspection. You mentally take yourself back to the particular point in the interview with which you are concerned (retrospection), and you try to examine, sentence by sentence, what the client said and what you said or did in response (introspection).

On another sheet of standard-size paper record your introspective/retrospective comments relevant to each intervention you made. Number these comments to agree with the numbers on the typescript. Thus, in annotating your sixth comment in the interview (w6) the annotation on the retrospective/introspective comment sheet should be labeled (w6).

Retrospective/introspective comments should include material on your affective reaction at the time, what you were feeling at that point in the interview, what you were thinking at that point in the interview, what prompted you to say what you say or do what you did at that point in the interview. If you can, try to include the theoretical explanation or justification for what you said or did. In justifying your choice of responses you should on occasion be able to refer to the social work literature in support: "I decided to do (this or that) because the research (or some authority, which you then cite) suggests that (this or that) is a desirable approach in situations of this kind."

The typescript of the tape and the retrospective/introspective comments should face each other so that you have page one of the typescript on the left and the first page of the retrospective comments on the right. The result should look something like this:

Page 1	Page 2
(Typescript of interview)	(Retrospective/introspective analysis)
C1.	W1. . . . .
C2.	W2. . . . .

Thus the odd-numbered pages of interview typescript face even-numbered pages of analysis.

Here is an excerpt from a completed assignment illustrating the nature of the analysis. The client is a 21-year-old, middle-income single woman who suspects that she is pregnant. She has had a continuing relationship with the father of the child. The excerpt is from the middle segment of the interview. The interviewer is a graduate social worker in a family service agency.

TRANSCRIPT	ANALYSIS

C19:

He told me, if there was anything he could do, *if* I was pregnant, he would help. I know that he's a respectable person. I just had a couple of days of doubt, and now I've received letters and phone calls, and I know where I stand again—with him.

W20:
Stand with him?

W20:
I am attempting to clarify what she means by "knowing where I stand."

C20:
I just don't know where I stand with my body.

W21:
Well, assuming, let's assume that you are pregnant. If you are pregnant, what would you want to do?

W21:
Once again I was trying to get her to focus, trying to simplify the issues for her and handle each problem individually. So I elected to focus on the pregnancy rather than the relationship to the father. I do this because she shifts the focus to her body. The purpose of my question is to learn what she wants to do and to clarify for myself what kind of referral she will need.

C21:
Well, I would like, he wanted me to tell him, I, I guess I could tell him…

W22:
You want to have an abortion?

W22:
This was a yes-no question, but I asked it purposely because I was trying to find out if she wanted an abortion or not. She had misunderstood my question in w21 and did not answer what she would want to do about the pregnancy itself. I may have come across as somewhat impatient here, but I also wanted to pull the interview into a tangible focus, which I think was good at this time.

C22:
Yes.

W23:
You don't want to keep the child?

C23:
No, I don't because, well, you can understand why. Any single girl can understand why. I want to have it

before it is in bodily form. I wouldn't want to get rid of—abort—a bodily form.

w24:
But you do want to wait until you know for sure you're pregnant?

c24:
Well, yes.

w25:
Rather than spending the money?

c25:
Yes, 'cause I don't have any money right now.

w26:
O.K.

c26:
Well, I can go on forever about why I can't be pregnant.

w23–26:
I asked a lot of yes-no questions here but felt they were necessary to find out what she was thinking and to help me understand what I could do for her. I was trying to find out whether she wanted an abortion. Does she want to determine whether she is pregnant before she has an abortion, or would it be easier for her if she were not sure? How does she feel about abortion? I thought I might be able to elicit her feelings if I kept on the track of what she would do about her pregnancy.

The next excerpt is from an interview with an adolescent in a foster care who recently had a falling out with her boyfriend Jeff and attempted suicide by taking sleeping pills. The interviewer is a social worker in a county welfare agency. The client has just said she feels depressed, sad, and very much alone.

TRANSCRIPT	ANALYSIS
W24 WORKER: Is that kinda how you were feeling when you took your foster mother's sleeping pills? Just were you feeling alone? Like you had nobody to talk to?	w24: "Took your mother's pills." I should have said "tried to commit suicide." I feel I have been denying and avoiding facing what this young girl has done. My discomfort also shows in providing her with answers to my question.
C25 CLIENT: Yeah—yeah, that's it exactly; that's how it was.	
W25 WORKER: What were some of your other feelings when you took the pills?	w25: This is good because it encourages the client to further discuss what

was behind her suicide attempt. Her thoughts are still all over the place, and the client is still overwhelmed by the feelings she had when she tried to commit suicide. I am trying to have her identify pieces of her depression so that the feelings do not seem so unmanageable.

C26 CLIENT:
I don't know. I guess, um, well, I'm just as, so confused I don't know what to do . . .

W26 WORKER:
What to do?

W26:
I am encouraging the client to continue talking. It might have been more effective to remain silent for a bit longer.

C27 CLIENT:
It's, um, like I don't know, like I said, I don't know. Like I said, Jeff's my life and I've kind of lost touch with a lot of my friends, um, 'cause Jeff and I have always been together and every night I went out, we went out . . . well, and when he isn't there, I don't really feel the need to go to other friends. I kind of feel like, well, I neglected my friends for two years, and now I can't expect them to listen to me bitch and moan.

W27 WORKER:
What kinds of things did you and Jeff do? What kinds of interests do you have?

W27:
This was a good example of not really listening or staying on task. Here it is essential to get her away from feeling that she can't go to her friends, and I got her off track because I thought helping her resolve her relationship with Jeff was more important. This is not a good transition.

C28 CLIENT:
Hmmm—Everything. We just had a lot of fun together, which is one thing we never do anymore. We just goof around, watch TV, and, um, just talk about everything. We have a lot of the same in school—in chemistry.

After you have written your retrospective/introspective analysis of the moment-to-moment interaction, answer the following questions:

How do you think you were perceived by the client?
What evidence supports your assessment?
How would you describe your overall attitude toward the client?
If you had the opportunity to do this interview again, what would you do differently? What reasons would you give for the changes you would make?

Suggestions for Taping the Interview Try to secure a quiet place free from traffic and office noise so that the taping will be clear.

You will get the best quality recording if you can use two microphones, one for you and one for the client. If the recorder has a jack that accepts only one microphone, or if you have only one microphone, place the one microphone between you and the client but nearer the client. You can remember to talk loudly and clearly, but you may not always be able to get the client to talk loudly and clearly. Consequently, it would be better to favor the client in positioning the microphone.

Set the recording volume up past midpoint but not at the highest volume level. Recording at the highest volume level leads to distortion.

If you can put the microphone on a folded handkerchief or cloth without being too fussy about it, do so. A table or a desk acts as a good sound conductor, and if you should tap the table, kick it, or set a coffee cup down on it, the sounds will record as loud clangs. For similar reasons it would be better to put the tape recorder on the floor rather than on a table or desk. It is also less obviously intrusive if it is out of the way.

Make certain that you are actually recording, that dials and knobs are set correctly. It would be sad to have conducted a good interview only to find that the recorder was not operating—which has happened on occasion.

Use a recording speed that permits at least forty-five minutes or more of recording without having to flip the cassette or change the reel. This interrupts the interview and is distracting. If what is required is not clear, please ask me for clarification. I'll be glad to discuss this with you.

Good luck on the assignment.

The Interview: Comments for the Instructor

Students have generally found the interview assignment to be one that has considerable learning potential. It forces students into a systematic step-by-step, intervention-by-intervention examination of their performance. The assignment helps them identify for themselves and to themselves some recurrent mistakes in interviewing. They often find that they are not doing what they assumed they were doing as a matter of course and that they are in fact doing things that impede the course of the interview.

The principal objection to the assignment is that it requires the time-consuming job of dogged typing. An hourlong interview, when transcribed, may run to thirty or thirty-five typed pages. Some interviews are of course shorter but still require considerable typing. If an interview runs for more than an hour, we modify the assignment by asking students to type and analyze the first ten minutes, the last ten minutes, and ten minutes of some midinterview segment.

Students often ask how long the interview should be. The answer is as long as the interview takes. Some interviews are completed in twenty minutes and are structurally coherent—they have a beginning, middle, and an end, and the purpose of the interview has been achieved.

Tell students that grading is based not on the interview but on the level of perception with which they analyze the interview. An extremely poor interview can suffice —if the student clearly identifies the elements that make it a poor interview and analyzes it coherently, the write-up should merit an *A*.

Assignment: The Term Paper

An alternative assignment for students who cannot interview a client, friend, or relative is a traditional term paper. The following is an example of a handout for such an assignment.

Instructions for a Term Paper (15–20 pp.)

1. Choose your topic wisely. The paper should be sharply focused. Because its length is limited, you do not have enough space to properly examine a broad topic (nonverbal interviewing, intrapersonal communications, etc.), and your paper is likely to be superficial. If your paper is to be acceptable as a scholarly effort, it should probe some question of limited scope in some detail. Titles such as "Interviewing the Resistive Client," "Uses of Confrontation in the Interview," and "Techniques for Making Interview Transitions" suggest the scope of acceptable paper topics.
2. The paper should show evidence of outside reading and research. It should contain bibliographical citations to outside readings. If you are doing a paper on some aspects of foster care, you will find it helpful to read a couple of books in the general area and then research the articles and studies of particular relevance to your selected area of focus.
3. Make an effort to orient the material to the practical concerns of social workers. This is a course in a professional school. Consequently, the pay-

off in doing the assignments is their relevance to the practice of social work, to the things you will be doing as a professional on the job in a few short months.

4. The paper should include your thinking, feelings, and reactions. What do you think and feel about the problem, the content area you have chosen to discuss? Your paper should not be an annotated bibliography that regurgitates, relatively unchanged, what you have read but an analytic synthesis that focuses on the topic you have chosen to explore.

5. The paper need not be a library exercise. It might be a discussion of some project, some service you are involved in (or become involved in for the purpose of the paper). In any case, you are asked not merely to be descriptive and expository but perceptively analytical. You should derive from your exploration some generalizations, and in each instance you should demonstrate your familiarity with the relevant literature. However, even if you are analyzing a personal experience, it is reasonable to suppose that other social workers have had similar experiences. Consequently, you should read and *cite* material from the social work literature relevant to your paper.

6. Any topic, problem, or question is acceptable so long as it is within the general confines of the ballpark—in this instance, the social work interview. If you have doubts about the acceptability of some topic, I would be happy to discuss this with you individually.

If you have difficulty finding a topic, I would be happy to discuss this with you individually. If you are clear about your interest and have no doubt about its relevance to interviewing but need help with suggestions for relevant reading, I would also be happy to discuss this with you individually. Good luck!

Sample Examination Questions

Instructors have different attitudes toward examinations. Humanistically oriented instructors tend to resist the idea. Examinations emphasize the hierarchical difference between student and instructor. They increase social distance between student and instructor and weaken attempts at colleagiality. They put instructors in a position of judge and evaluator, which is contrary to the image instructors might have of their relationship with students.

Some instructors feel that examinations have considerable educational value. Exams motivate students to study the material systematically. They stimulate a review of the material so that students can see different units of the course in perspective, thus strengthening the integration and continuity of units. Examinations give students feedback, making them explicitly aware of their weaknesses in interviewing and what needs further study.

Aside from its educational potential, the examination is seen by some instructors as a recurring component in discharging their responsibility to the college and the community. Although a diploma at the end of training shows successful overall completion of work done, a good mark at the end of a course proves that the student has achieved some proficiency in the subject matter of the course. In granting such certification, the instructor has to have confidence in an objective measure of student proficiency. An examination is one way to provide such assurance.

Students also tend to be ambivalent about exams. Exams are difficult to live with, yet students miss them when exams are not given. Students have a strong need to know where they stand in the course. It is not always clear to them whether their performance is acceptable. Without exams or some kind of regular systematic feedback, students are left with an unnerving sense of uncertainty—which is distressing.

Whether to give exams or not is an instructor's prerogative. For those who are interested in giving an examination, we have listed questions in a variety of formats.

The variety of questions is suggestive of the different question formats that you might use. Instructors can and should imaginatively delete and add questions to the battery of questions suggested. Such additions and deletions would enable you to keep the examination maximally congruent with the content you actually taught in the course.

True or False

Mark the following statements either T (True) or F (False).

1. Good interview rapport is almost assured when a client requests an interview without coercion.
2. It is sometimes necessary to require clients to supply information, even though they may be reticent or uncooperative.
3. The interview has been found to be a valid method of determining a person's intelligence.
4. More failures in the interview result from lack of social and personal understandings than from lack of technical skills and abilities.
5. Ordinarily, the personal interview should last only twenty to thirty minutes.
6. In most guidance or counseling centers the first interview with a client is usually called the *intake interview*.

7. Each time a worker talks with a client, the conversation between them should come under the classification of *interview*.
8. The interview should not end without having the interviewer politely point out where the subject has erred and how to overcome the mistakes.
9. Carl Rogers sees certain advantages in drawing out the counselees by asking direct key questions.
10. Interviewers should take notes while interviewing so they do not to forget important points in the written report.
11. Interview information must often be supplemented with more objective data from other counseling techniques.
12. Patience and sympathetic understanding are usually considered requisites of a capable interviewer.
13. The preferred method of personal counseling is a frank and cooperative relationship between the interviewer and the interviewee.
14. Workers should meet with each of their clients only by a prearranged schedule.
15. It is advisable for the worker to be prepared to ask certain directly related questions in a predetermined way.
16. If, after a reasonable effort, rapport has not been established, the interviewer should proceed with the drawing-out phase of the interview.
17. It is best to conclude each interview with some words of positive encouragement such as, "Everything will be all right."
18. Knowledge of the client's physical condition, medical history, family background, and such will often contribute to the success of an interview.
19. Interviewing procedures may provide both therapeutic and diagnostic value in some instances.
20. It is best for counselors to be busy for a few minutes after the client enters the office, to enable the client to become accustomed to the surroundings.
21. The interview method may be used as a motivating device.
22. By making the line of questioning quite direct, the counselor is more apt to instill confidence in clients and gain their cooperation.
23. Results of statistical studies made to date have shown that interviewing methods have high reliability.
24. Sports, hobbies, and other casual topics are suitable for conversation about common interests, which builds better rapport.
25. If you are positive of your point of view and its benefits to clients, it is your duty to attempt to convince them of the merits of your suggestion.
26. Interviewing becomes successively easier when the subject returns three or four times, for by then rapport is automatically established.

27. The personal interview should always be held in an atmosphere of privacy.
28. Workers should attempt to avoid discussing problems with clients until they can come to the office.
29. The interviewer should always take an objective but cordial attitude toward the subject.
30. The reactions and expressions of clients may be as important for understanding them as their verbal responses.
31. The experienced interviewer should systematically evolve a set of valid and reliable questions for use in securing positive responses in a majority of problem situations.
32. Counselors can be certain that rapport has been established whenever individuals talk freely about their problems.
33. A positive relationship is a necessary but not sufficient condition for effective interviewing.
34. The content and direction of the interview are controlled by the interviewer to achieve the interviewer's purpose.
35. The worker engages in "brokerage" and "advocacy" to develop positive relationships between social agencies.
36. We often hear what we want to hear rather than what was actually said.
37. The best way to check whether the interviewer has received the message correctly is to ask the interviewee. This is called *reflecting*.
38. The interview, like other professional relationships, is designed to be nondirectional in the help offered.
39. One disadvantage of home visits is that interaction between family members is distracting to the interview.
40. Open questions usually start with *what* and *when*; closed questions usually start with *did* and *how*.
41. Open questions should be followed by probes to clarify the nature of the client's situation.
42. We can generally listen faster than people can talk.
43. Questioning a client's lie threatens a good relationship.
44. A competent interviewer is more attentive to verbal cues than to nonverbal cues.
45. The relationship between hearing and listening is similar to the relationship between sensing and perceiving.
46. Interviewing is merely organized conversation.
47. In interviewing children reported as suspected of being sexually abused it is best to assume that children never lie.
48. Nonverbal events are meaningful only in the context in which they occur.
49. The "funnel approach" in interviewing means moving from specific questions to broader general questions.

50. *Artifactual communication* refers to the changing distances between interview participants.
51. Preconceived attitudes toward other people help us to listen to them because we have an indication of what they are likely to say.
52. Clients should not be encouraged to openly express critical and/or hostile feelings about the worker.
53. The direction of concern in the interview should be unilateral and not reciprocal.
54. The purpose of the interview should not influence the method the worker uses to conduct the interview.
55. A social worker should refrain at all times from giving advice.
56. Client self-determination is an absolute right.
57. A client who cannot make eye contact with the interviewer is probably lying.
58. Good interviewers maintain intense eye-to-eye contact at all times.
59. It is most important to offer solutions to a client's problems as soon as possible in the interview.
60. A competent interviewer is comfortable with brief reflective silences.

Sentence Completion

Please complete the following sentences:

1. A positive relationship is a _____ but not

   _____ condition for an effective interview.

2. An interview is a _____ with a specific

   _____.

3. The content and direction of the interview is the responsibility of the

   _____ in order to achieve the

   _____ of the interview.

4. The interview is designed to serve the interests of the _____

   _____.

5. Unlike social conversation, _____ sometimes

   requires the discussion of _____ subjects.

6. We should limit our explanation of knowledge about the client

_____ to that information necessary

to_____ the _____ of

the interview.

7. To ensure that the client understands a communication, the worker must choose not only suitable vocabulary but also must consider the client's _____.

8. Messages are filtered and screened by recipients when accurate interpretation of the message would make them feel _____.

9. We attribute characteristics to the interviewee that are typical for the _____ with which we perceive the interviewee to be affected. This is called _____.

10. We check our understanding of a message by asking for _____
_____.

11. The term *relationship* in social work refers to the _____ between people.

12. A worker should strive to be consistently _____ rather than consistently popular.

13. We often hear what we _____ rather than what is said.

14. The interviewer is likely to influence the interviewee more than the reverse because the interviewer has more _____.

15. Expressions of interest by the interviewer such as "Uh-huh," "I see," and "Go on," are experienced by the interviewee as _____.

16. In using the techniques of reflection it is important to avoid _____
_____clients' thoughts for them.

17. The best interpretation is one that is most clearly _____
_____ by the interviewee.

18. Questioning often moves from the more _____ to the more _____.

19. To obtain more specific information about the client's situation, the interviewer may have to ask a series of _____ questions.

20. When changing to a new topic, the worker should _____ _____ the intention to make the transition.

21. Leading questions are particularly undesirable with children because children are highly _____.

22. Nonverbal events are meaningful only in the _____ in which they occur.

23. Disclosures by the interviewer are likely to encourage _____ _____ by the interviewee.

24. Interviewees feel forced to share information about themselves if you communicate _____ understanding.

25. In order to be _____ in the interview, interviewers needs to know their own values and have a sense of self-awareness.

26. Being accepting means accepting the _____ but not necessarily the _____.

27. Pointing out in an accepting manner the discrepancies in the behavior of the interviewee is called _____.

28. Kinesics, paralinguistics, and artifacts are examples of _____ _____ communication.

29. The interviewer who manifests an awareness of racial and ethnic differences is manifesting _____ sensitivity.

30. Listening is _____ from _____.

31. The best way to start an interview with a client is _____

    _____.

32. Taking extensive notes during an interview is an undesirable procedure

    because _____.

33. Motivating the client to actively participate in the interview can be

    achieved by _____.

34. One important advantage of interviewing the client at home is that

    _____.

35. In terminating an interview it is desirable for the interviewer to

    _____.

36. The seating arrangement that in most instances is conducive to good

    interviewing is one in which the interviewer sits _____

    _____.

37. The interviewer needs to have a good firm knowledge of the subject

    matter content of the interview because _____.

38. A response in which workers relate something personal about them-

    selves is called _____.

39. A response that points out verbal discrepancies is called _____

    _____.

40. A response that uses inferences is called_____

    _____.

Matching

For each interviewer response listed identify the technique best illustrated by this response:

_____

CLIENT: I guess I don't trust other women that much. I'm always competing
with them for something.

INTERVIEWER RESPONSE:		TECHNIQUE:
_____	1. You say you compete with women. How do you react to men?	a. Giving advice
_____	2. Are you afraid that other women might be more attractive than you?	b. Expressing feelings
_____	3. Describe to me the last time you found yourself competing with another woman.	c. Interpreting d. Reflecting
_____	4. Imagine you were in a group interview for a job that was important to you. Try to tell me what your feelings would be.	e. Minimal encouraging f. Topical shift
_____	5. So what you're saying is that you find it difficult to trust other women and have often found yourself competing with them.	g. Criticizing h. Seeking concreteness
_____	6. I think you'd feel a lot more comfortable if you gave women more of a chance.	i. Interrupting
_____	7. Competing?	j. Constructive confrontation
_____	8. But you have strong feelings of affection for a number of women in your life. That seems to contradict what you are saying.	k. Summarizing
_____	9. Hearing this makes me feel a bit frustrated.	
_____	10. As I see it, you've had several experiences with women that have led you to distrust most of them and you also see yourself competing with them at work and socially. Is that correct?	

Identifying Interview Interventions

Listed here are a number of statements made by interviewees. Each statement is followed by four interviewer responses. Use the list of seven interviewer interventions that follows to identify one of the four responses to each interaction. The response that you choose to identify should be the one that you think meets the definition of one of the seven interventions listed.

INTERVIEWER INTERVENTIONS:

1. Clarification
2. Interpretation
3. Minimal encouragement
4. Paraphrase
5. Summarizing
6. Reflection
7. Advice/suggestion

1. INTERVIEWEE: I have been trying to get a job, but it is hard to find something I like and has a future, and my parents are getting impatient. They're not particularly happy about having a 29-year-old son at home and they act it.

INTERVIEWER: a. I would imagine so.
b. Which?
c. It's not likely to make you feel good.
d. Good jobs, as you say, are hard to come by.

2. INTERVIEWEE: Now that I've gone back to school, my husband complains that I don't have any time to spend with him or the kids and that I am always tired, and the housework doesn't get done.

INTERVIEWER: a. Does it seem to you that maybe going back to school was not such a good decision?
b. Have you discussed with your husband his becoming more active in the care of the house and the kids?
c. I think I know how you feel because when I went back to school I had some of the sameproblems.
d. So, going back to school seems to have created some problems in relation to your husband,your contact with your children, and your responsbilities around the care of the house.

3. INTERVIEWEE: Like we discussed last time, I'd really like to be more assertive. But this week, after a long day and everybody had gone, my boss asked me to do something at the last minute as I was starting to leave, and I did it.

INTERVIEWER: a. Do you think your boss was right to ask you?
b. Could you tell me more about what he asked you to do?
c. It seems to me there is a discrepancy between your desire to be assertive and your actual be-

havior. Could you help me understand this discrepancy?

    d. How do you think you might have felt if you had said no?

4. INTERVIEWEE: Okay, I haven't been the best daughter—dropping out of school, getting into drugs, shoplifting. But my parents haven't been the best kind of parents. I have been physically and sexually abused and felt rejected all along. And now they know I am pregnant and I am glad of it.

    INTERVIEWER: a. While you did what you did, you feel your parents are somewhat to blame.

    b. You seem clear about how you feel about your parents. I might be wrong, but could it be that your pregnancy is a way of getting back at your parents?

    c. Have you had any kind of exam to confirm that you actually are pregnant?

    d. Perhaps we need to discuss today whether you want to abort the pregnancy or carry the child to term and consider adoption.

5. INTERVIEWEE: We would like to have a child, but it would mean that my wife would have to give up her job just when we need more income. But neither one of us is getting younger, and biologically it may soon become more difficult if we delay.

    INTERVIEWER: a. It seems to me you are ambivalent about this. On the one hand, you are getting more anxious about your age, but on the other hand, you recognize some of the difficulties of having a child. You're pulled in two directions at once.

    b. Have you talked to your wife about your pro and con feelings about parenthood?

    c. As you weigh the alternatives in your mind, does the decision in one direction weigh more heavily than the decision in the other direction, or are they about equally balanced?

    d. I hear you struggling with a very personal decision, and I am glad you had the courage to raise it for discussion.

6. INTERVIEWEE [*An elderly widower*]: I seem to be managing [*looking off with inflection in his voice*]. I take care of the house and the dog, and I get out some with my

friends [*his hands folded and body slightly stooped*]. I am managing pretty well, generally.

INTERVIEWER:
  a. I am pleased to hear that you are managing so well. That's good.

  b. I hear you say you're managing, but your voice and your actions seem to suggest that things may not be going so well. Could it be that you're still feeling sad and depressed?

  c. You get out with your friends. Could you tell me more about that?

7. INTERVIEWEE: Well, I lost my job, couldn't get another one, and the family budget went to pot, making things more difficult between myself and my wife so that she made good on a frequent threat to get a divorce, and now we are separated.

INTERVIEWER:
  a. That's one bad blow after the other, more stress than most people can take.

  b. The loss of the job led to several difficulties that increased conflict between you and your wife resulting in divorce, and now you are alone.

  c. Given all that pile of trouble, I can understand why you might need to come for help at this time.

  d. From your description of the situation it doesn't seem likely that you and your wife can get back together, does it?

8. INTERVIEWEE: Things seem to go from bad to worse, and I get so depressed that I feel, what's the use of trying?

INTERVIEWER:
  a. Things seem to be so difficult that you don't feel it's worth making the effort to try to do anything to change the situation.

  b. I think I can understand how you feel, because it is a difficult situation.

  c. But unless you make the effort, things are not likely to get better—isn't that so?

  d. Well, I know many people who have been in your situation, and we have been successful in helping them.

9. INTERVIEWEE: I think I am confused about where we are going with these interviews. I am not sure I see how this is going to help me solve my problems.

INTERVIEWER:
  a. I think as you go along you might find the relevance of your problems to what we are doing.

      b. Could you tell me more specifically what you find confusing about what we are doing?

      c. I realize it is complicated, but I can assure you we know what we are doing. We have a lot of experience with this.

      d. I know many people like you have also found the experience confusing at this point in the contact.

10. INTERVIEWEE: So, after he gives me all these bruises, he goes through his old song-and-dance, like he's sorry and he's never going to do it again—the whole old business. I don't know.

INTERVIEWER: a. Well, he's done this before.

      b. Sorry to hear that.

      c. It seems that it might be time to consider leaving.

      d. He is persistent.

Multiple Choice

Check the best answer in each of the following:

1. In the case of an interview in which the client immediately and angrily makes a series of critical statements about the agency and the worker, the best procedure on the part of the worker would probably be to

    _____   a. Disregard the anger until the client has released the angry feelings.

    _____   b. Terminate the interview.

    _____   c. Postpone the matter until the interviewer can come back with a supervisor.

    _____   d. Attempt to convince the client that he is wrong.

2. If in the course of an interview, the client avoids a certain topic or changes the course of the conversation when the topic is mentioned, the worker should

    _____   a. Insist on returning to the topic.

    _____   b. Try to use the avoidance to determine the reason for it and its significance.

    _____   c. Ask why the client is avoiding the topic.

    _____   d. Determine that it has no importance.

3. While conducting an interview, it is considered best if the worker

_____   a. Takes extensive notes.

_____   b. Takes no notes.

_____   c. Asks the client to write down all important facts.

_____   d. Takes notes only of important facts not easily remembered, such as names and addresses.

4. Social work interviewing is always directed to the client and the client's situation. The following statements address the proper focus of an interview. Pick the one you think is most accurate:

_____   a. The worker limits the client to concentration on objective data.

_____   b. The client is generally permitted to talk about facts and feelings with no direction from the worker.

_____   c. The main focus in social work interviews is on feelings rather than facts.

_____   d. The worker is responsible for helping the client focus on any material that seems to be related to the client's problems or difficulties.

5. In a training program you discuss the problem of interviewing a dull client who gives a slow and disconnected case history. Select from the following the procedure that you would recommend as most likely to help the worker obtain the necessary information in this case.

_____   a. Ask the client leading questions requiring yes or no answers.

_____   b. Ask the client to limit narration to the essential facts so that the interview can be as brief as possible.

_____   c. Review the story with the client, patiently asking simple questions.

_____   d. State that unless the client becomes more cooperative, you cannot help solve the problem.

6. *Structuring* means

_____   a. Clarifying the roles of worker and client.

_____ b. Bringing out the emotional problems of the client.

_____ c. Clarifying the problems involved in the case in the worker's report.

_____ d. Clarifying the problems involved in the case in the client's mind.

7. The best way to start an interview with a client is to

_____ a. Immediately plunge into the business of the visit.

_____ b. Let the client determine whether to get down to business immediately.

_____ c. Make the interview a social call before getting down to business.

_____ d. Let each case "stand on its own feet" in determining how to proceed.

8. The best response of the unmarried childless interviewer, when asked by a client if she is married and has children, is to say,

_____ a. What prompts you to ask?

_____ b. I would like to devote all our time together trying to help you rather than discussing my situation.

_____ c. I am not married and don't have children.

_____ d. What difference would it make to you if I weren't married or a parent?

9. If the client appears unable to stop talking, the worker should

_____ a. Terminate the interview.

_____ b. Allow the client to talk until finished.

_____ c. Ask for only yes or no answers.

_____ d. In some way proceed to control the interview.

10. Of the following factors in an interview, the most difficult for the worker to control is

_____ a. The interest of the client.

_____ b. The objectivity of the worker's mental attitudes.

_____   c. The tendency of the client to want to take up too much time.

_____   d. The tendency of other members of the family to interfere.

11 The best way for a worker to elicit hard-to-get information from a client is to

_____   a. Explain carefully why the information is needed.

_____   b. Demand that the client answer all questions with yes or no.

_____   c. Work around to the subject from a new direction.

_____   d. Tell the client that failing to give the information will result in future difficulty in dealing with the agency.

12. The chief basis for the inability of a troubled client to express a problem clearly to the worker is that the client

_____   a. Sees the problem in complex terms and does not think it possible to give the worker the whole picture.

_____   b. Has erected defenses against emotions that seem to the client to be inadmissible or intolerable.

_____   c. Cannot describe how she feels about the problem.

_____   d. Views the situation as unlikely to be solved and is blocked in self-expression.

13. A person, such as an employer, whom a worker interviews in regard to a client, is termed

_____   a. Corroborative.

_____   b. Collateral.

_____   c. Accessory.

_____   d. Secondary.

14. When the interviewer and client are able to discuss the client's problems with mutual understanding and without conflict, the situation usually is referred to as:

_____   a. Adjustment.

_____   b. Rapport.

_____   c. Cooperation.

_____   d. Social harmony.

15. Of the subjects that might be discussed by a client in an initial interview
     with a social worker, the most important is (are) the

_____   a. Functions of the agency and its importance to the client.

_____   b. Opinions of the worker about the client's home situation.

_____   c. Extent of the client's need for the services of the agency.

_____   d. Future contacts that will be made between the client and
                 the worker.

16. An example of a poor listening habit is

_____   a. Nodding your head when you agree.

_____   b. Mentally reviewing what the speaker has just said.

_____   c. Thinking about the next statement you want to make.

_____   d. Trying to understand the main ideas instead of just re-
                 membering the facts.

17. A leading question is on that leads

_____   a. To the preferred answer.

_____   b. Into the body of an interview.

_____   c. To further questions.

_____   d. Into a persuasive interview.

18. Which of the following statements indicates empathic listening?

_____   a. I know what you mean—the same thing happened to me
                 last year. Now, here's how to handle the problem.

_____   b. I'm sorry you feel bad. I hate to see nice people like you
                 have problems.

_____   c. I know you're upset, but it isn't my fault that you failed the
                 test—you're the one that didn't study.

_____ d. I felt lonely my first year in school too. I think you are saying that you need more friends.

19. If you begin an interview with broad open questions and then ask questions that are increasingly restrictive and more closed, you are using the interview organizational pattern known as the

_____ a. Funnel approach.

_____ b. Pyramid approach.

_____ c. Hourglass approach.

_____ d. Tube approach.

20. Listening and hearing are different because

_____ a. Listening involves reception, whereas hearing involves perception.

_____ b. Listening is learned, whereas hearing is natural.

_____ c. Listening is perceptive, whereas hearing is selective.

_____ d. Hearing is learned, whereas listening is natural.

Rating Interview Responses

Excerpts from a Social Work Interview

The client's comment is followed by three responses by the worker. Select the response you think is most appropriate. And in the space given, tell why you think the response you have selected is the best.

If you are dissatisfied with **all three** *responses provided, write what you would have said in response to the client's comments. And in the space given, tell why you think the response you have formulated is the best one.*

Background on Interview

Mr. R., living alone in a small two-bedroom home, is receiving agency help that supplements OASI payments. He is 68 and recently retired from his job as a semiskilled worker in a shoe factory; he began work at the factory after he injured his back lifting a heavy load. His wife died two years ago. He has two children—a son who is 34, married, the father of four children, and employed as a bus driver, and a daughter who is 30, married, the mother of three children, and employed as a rural mail carrier.

This is the worker's third visit to the client, who has called the worker and requested the visit.

---

1. CLIENT: I am sorry if I troubled you any in asking you to come to see me. I don't like it, having to ask for anything, I mean.

    WORKER:

    a. It's all right—it's our job trying to help people, and I was coming out this way anyhow. There is a client I have to see near here.

    b. It's perfectly okay. What did you want to see me about?

    c. You don't have to feel uncomfortable about asking to see me. I would like to be of some help to you if there is something troubling you.

    d. _____

    Reasons for selection made: _____

---

2. CLIENT: The reason I wanted to see you is that I just can't get along on what I get.

    WORKER:

    a. Mmm—hmm.

    b. I'm sorry to hear that. It must be hard for you.

    c. How do you think we can be of help to you?

    d. _____

    Reasons for selection made: _____

---

3. CLIENT: I always used to be able to manage pretty well and raised a family on a kinda small income. Here I am all alone now with no one but myself to look after, and I just can't seem to be able to make out.

    WORKER:

    a. You're having quite a bit of trouble with the budget, and you're wondering why that is?

    b. You seem to have been a good manager all along. What seems to you to be the trouble now?

    c. You seem to be having trouble with the budget. Do you think it's because you don't understand the budget or because the allotment is too small?

    d. _____

Reasons for selection made: _____

_____

4. There's a lot of things I need that don't seem covered in the budget somehow. Like it's not easy to visit my grandchildren without bringing a little something.

    WORKER:

    a. Yeah, I guess you're right. There are some things that seem important to you but are not covered in the budget. Were there any other things you find yourself spending money for and are not covered in the budget?

    b. Well, we can only allow those things that are permitted by the department. I think you can understand that we can't include every item in the budget, and presents or candy for grandchildren are not included.

    c. That does seem a shame, and I wish we could allow such things in the budget, but we can't according to department rules.

    d. _____

Reasons for selection made: _____

_____

5. **CLIENT:** I don't think you people realize how it is to be living here all alone, so if I have to go out for a beer or maybe to a movie to break up the loneliness, I can't because the amount I have to live on is so small.

    WORKER:

    a. I have many clients who are senior citizens like yourself living alone, so I think I do understand the problem you face.

    b. Being lonely is a hard thing, as you say, and I guess a limited budget isn't much of a help. I wonder if you have ever given any thought to the activities of the Golden Age Club?

    c. You may be right in what you're saying and in the way you feel about it. The budgetary limits are something both you and I have to accept as a reality, and I don't think there is much we can do about it. I guess you realize that, don't you?

d. _____

Reasons for selection made: _____

_____

6. CLIENT: You would think my kids would visit with me more or try to take me out or give me some extra money. But I guess when you get to be my age, everybody forgets and nobody cares about you, and you might as well be dead.

    WORKER:

    a. I am sure your children think about you often, and if they don't take you out or help you more, it's because they have responsibilities to their own families.

    b. The agency does care about what happens to you and would like to help.

    c. You think your family has let you down.

    d. _____

Reasons for selection made: _____

_____

The following vignettes suggest an alternative form of the same type of multiple choice examination.

For each of the following vignettes, check the response that you think is most appropriate, most desirable.

    1. You are a school social worker, and a 10-year-old boy has been directed by the principal to talk with you because he was caught smoking pot in the lavatory. You have been told that the boy thinks there is nothing wrong

with this and that marijuana should be decriminalized. Which of the following would be your best opening?

_____   a. "I think I can understand your feelings. I used to smoke some pot myself."

_____   b. "How do you feel about being asked to see me?"

_____   c. "I know you didn't come to see me voluntarily but since you're here, how do you think we can be of help?"

_____   d. "We have about a half-hour together. What would you like to talk about?

2. A report of suspected abuse has been received, and you have been assigned to the case. In response to your appearance at the home the mother asks with some annoyance and irritation, "Who are you?"

_____   a. "My name is _____.
           I represent Child Protective Services, and I have come to investigate a report of suspected child abuse."

_____   b. "I am from a community agency that receives reports about families that might need help in caring for their children."

_____   c. "I recognize that you might be upset about a stranger knocking at your door, but I am obligated to discuss with you a report about your abuse of your child."

_____   d. "We are concerned about what is best for you and your child and would like to talk to you about this. May I come in?"

3. The client is a 47-year-old woman whom you are interviewing as a worker in a family service agency. This is the first interview, and the client, who has been talking freely about her marital problem, has just said, "I'll tell you how I see this." In the slight pause that follows, you say,

_____   a. "How do *you* see this?"

_____   b. "How does it look to you, eh?"

_____   c. "Uh-huh.

_____   d. "I see."

4. You are interviewing a middle-aged woman whose 83-year-old mother had been referred to a nursing home but who insisted on returning to live with her daughter (the interviewee). The interviewee has just said, "She doesn't let us do anything—she won't let us alone to read or to watch TV and she follows us around all the time. We need some freedom."

Which of the following would be the most appropriate response?

_____ a. "You feel she's a burden on the family."

_____ b. "Why do you think she does that?"

_____ c. "What didn't she like about the nursing home?"

_____ d. "You need some breathing space."

5. A neighbor has called to report a case of child abuse. She hears the mother hollering and hitting her 6-year-old boy with a strap. She has seen bruises on the hands and face of the child. In taking the report over the phone you have asked the informant for her name and address. The caller replies, "Why do you want my name?" Select the best answer among the following options. You may think none of the options is desirable; if that is the case, write what you might have answered.

_____ a. "Because I may have to contact you again about the information you have shared with us."

_____ b. "Because the parent who is being reported has a right to know."

_____ c. "We may need to get more information from you about this."

_____ d. "Because you're the one who knows about the situation, and we may need your help."

Interview Completions

Please complete the following interactions:

1. You are a social worker at County Social Services. This is the first interview with a young woman who has come to your agency for assistance in managing her household affairs. She was recently separated from her husband and is responsible for the care of her three small children. You ask her, "Do you have enough money to buy necessities for you and the children?" She replies, uncertainly, "Oh, I guess so." You say, _____

2. You are a probation worker with the Division of Corrections. Your client is a man in his late 20s who has recently been released from state prison and is looking for a job. He has been complaining about how badly he has been treated at the employment office and says, "They just don't even try once they see you've got a record." You say, _____

_____

3. You are a hospital social worker. Your client is a young woman who had been admitted to the hospital with broken ribs and other minor injuries. This is your first interview. Your client has been telling you how her husband abuses her. She suddenly bursts into tears and says, "Oh, he's so hateful, isn't he? That dirty bastard, I'll fix him." You say, _____

_____

4. You are a social worker with a neighborhood center. Your adolescent client is in trouble with the police. This is the third time he has been picked up for joy riding. You have seen him many times. He says, "It wasn't my fault. The other guys sort of started it, and I couldn't do anything but go along with them." You say, _____

_____

5. You are a social worker at a mental health clinic. This is the third interview with this client, a middle-aged man whom you have been seeing because of his depression. In the previous two interviews you noticed that he seemed to blame many things on his mother, who has at this point been dead for four years. Your client is now blaming his recent job loss on his mother and says, "If only she had disciplined me more!" You say, _____

_____

6. You are a social worker at a school for girls (state correctional facility). This is your first interview with a 17-year-old resident who is new to the institution. She has a history of drug addiction and is visibly pregnant. You are asking her to tell you her thoughts about being in this new facility, and she says, "I just can't communicate with anyone. We talk but we don't communicate." You say, _____

_____

7. You are a social worker at the County Mental Health Clinic. Your client is a middle-aged woman you have been seeing regularly for the past six months. She has been very depressed and since you saw her last made

an unsuccessful suicide attempt. She says, "You know how miserable my life has been lately. You must understand why I tried to kill myself and why I just don't find life worth living anymore. What's the use in going on? I have nothing to live for anymore." You say,_____

_____

8. You are a new social worker at a drug abuse treatment center. You have been assigned Mr. Brown's caseload, because Mr. Brown recently resigned and went to another agency. Your client is a young woman who has seen Mr. Brown on three previous occasions. This is your first interview with her and you have just introduced yourself. She says abruptly, "But how can I trust you? I liked Mr. Brown and trusted him, but I just don't think I'll be able to talk to you at all." You say, _____

_____

9. You are a social worker who works with families of patients who are hospitalized in a psychiatric ward. Your client is the wife of a schizophrenic patient whose condition has improved enough that he can go home. The purpose of this interview is to prepare the wife for her husband's return home, and you are midway through the interview when your client, who seems fearful, says, "I really think he should stay a little longer in the hospital. The added rest will do him good. No sense rushing things. Don't you think it would be better if he stayed here longer?" You say, _____

_____

10. You are a social worker with Protective Services. Your client is a young single mother who has been reported for leaving her baby alone at night. This is your first interview, and you are attempting to explain the purpose of the meeting. You say, "We want to make sure that your baby is being well taken care of and offer you any assistance you might need." She blurts out, "Well, what business is it of yours? She's my baby and I'll take care of her the way I want to." You say, _____

_____

Specific Content Questions

Answer the following questions as directed:

1. List two different kinds of vocal communication, as distinguished from verbal communication.

a. _____

b. _____

2. List two characteristics that tend to distinguish the social work interview from the public opinion poll interview.

a. _____

b. _____

3. Define briefly two of these three terms: *acceptance, empathic understanding, self-determination.*

a. _____

b. _____

4. List two values of the judicious use of humor in an interview.

a. _____

b. _____

5. List two functions in the interview that the interviewer is required to perform.

a. _____

b. _____

6. List two different kinds of nonverbal activity in which interviewers would engage if they were attempting to communicate interest in the interviewee.

a. _____

b. _____

7. List two important things a worker might do in preparing for a scheduled interview.

a. _____

b. _____

8. List two factors that make for difficulty in good listening in the interview. (The question is directed at good listening, as distinguished from good hearing.)

a. _____

b. _____

9. List two procedures for making good smooth transitions in an interview.

a. _____

b. _____

10. List two problems that are encountered in interviewing many clients of 70 years of age or older.

a. _____

b. _____

11. List two factors that clearly distinguish an interview from a conversation.

a. _____

b. _____

12. List one advantageous result of matching interviewer and interviewee in terms of some significant cultural variable (African-American interviewer with African-American client; gay interviewer with gay client, etc.), and one disadvantage of such matching.

a. Advantage: _____

b. Disadvantage: _____

13. It is said that nonverbal communication might amplify, emphasize, anticipate, contradict, and/or accent the verbal message. Describe a nonverbal response that an interviewee might display in communicating any two of the five messages.

a. _____

b. _____

14. List two aspects of telephone interviews that make them different from face-to-face interviews.

a. _____

b. _____

15. List two approaches to the involuntary client that are likely to increase cooperativeness in the interview.

a. _____

b. _____

16. List two interviewing precautions that need to be observed in interviewing children reported as sexually abused.

a. _____

b. _____

17. Interviewees evoke many kinds of feelings in the interviewer, some of which tend to create problems. List two ways in which the interviewer might deal with problematic feelings evoked by the interviewee.

a. _____

b. _____

18. List three differences between experienced and inexperienced interviewers.

a. _____

b. _____

c. _____

19. List three characteristics of the culturally sensitive interviewer.

a. _____

b. _____

c. _____

20. List two ways you can communicate respect nonverbally.

a. _____

b. _____

21. List three things you might do to reduce the resistance of an involuntary interviewee.

a. _____

b. _____

c. _____

22. List four different ways we communicate nonverbally.

    a. _____

    b. _____

    c. _____

    d. _____

23. List three differences between a conversation and an interview.

    a. _____

    b. _____

    c. _____

24. List two types of transitions.

    a. _____

    b. _____

25. List three barriers to communication.

    a. _____

    b. _____

    c. _____

Essay Questions

1. Discuss barriers to effective interpersonal communication.
2. Discuss the difference between a conversation and an interview.
3. Discuss the adaptations in interviewing of which you need to be aware in interviewing minority group clients.
4. Mrs. M., age 36, called and requested an interview with a worker at the family service agency (or community mental health center). Information obtained by the receptionist over the phone included the following: Mr. and Mrs. M., both high school graduates, have been married for ten years. They have two children, Mary, 9, and Bill, 7, and they own their home. Mr. M., 38, is a welder and has worked steadily since their marriage. Mrs. M. has some word-processing skills and worked for three years before marriage but has not worked since then. Mrs. M. indicated she was considering a divorce but would like to discuss her general marital situation with somebody. An appointment

was made with you, and the receptionist has told you that Mrs. M. is in the waiting room.

You greet Mrs. M., help her to get settled, and exchange some general pleasantries. You are now ready to start the interview. Write the first five minutes as you imagine they unfolded. This would involve some six to eight interchanges (I said, Mrs. M. said). In each case state what prompted you to say what you said, ask what you asked, do what you did.

5. [At the last class meeting before the exam the instructor distributes the verbatim typescript of an extended interview. The students are instructed to read the typescript before the exam and to be prepared to answer questions on the interview. The exam questions on the typescript follow.]

Using the typescript of the interview distributed on the last day of class:

   a. Identify three examples of what you regard as *good* interviewing techniques as exhibited by the worker in the interview. For each of the three instances selected, explain briefly (two or three sentences) your reason(s) for selecting this as an example of *good* interviewing.

   b. Identify three examples of what you regard as *poor* interviewing techniques as exhibited by the worker in the interview. For each instance selected, explain briefly your reason for selecting this as an example of poor interviewing, and state briefly what you would have said or done at this point in the interview if you had been the interviewer.